DAUGHTER
OF A
PREACHER MAN

DAUGHTER OF A PREACHER MAN

A ROAD LESS TRAVELED

ANNA PICARD

authorHOUSE®

AuthorHouse™
1663 Liberty Drive
Bloomington, IN 47403
www.authorhouse.com
Phone: 1-800-839-8640

First published by AuthorHouse   11/30/2011

ISBN: 978-1-4634-0682-0 (sc)
ISBN: 978-1-4634-0681-3 (hc)
ISBN: 978-1-4634-0680-6 (ebk)

Library of Congress Control Number: 2011908240

Printed in the United States of America

CONTENTS

DEDICATION

This work is dedicated to all those who have supported me through the good and bad. I am thankful to my grandparents and parents who have been patient with me throughout the years. I am forever grateful for the loving support of my relatives and friends who have cheered me on through this difficult and challenging project. I am eternally thankful to my husband and daughter for their patience and hours of sacrifice, while I have labored through this project of love for you. All glory, honor and praise belong to Jesus.

FOREWORD

This is a '***must read***' book especially for the many in ministry and public life. One can push aside "The Road Less Traveled" as another account of a disgruntled or misguided preacher's child. To fulfill purpose and the desire to maximize our calling, children and family members silently go through traumas, hurts and various emotions. Often we take for granted that these "little ones" should have 'understood', realizing our error too late. On reading my daughter's personal diary now printed, jerked me into the 'reality' of being '***sold out.***' Relentless in my pursuit of changing lives for the better, and bringing hope to the hopeless, now causes introspection and self-examination. How did I not hear the soulful cries of my own children? Did I overlook their pain and take their acquiescence to this way of life, for granted?

Pastors, elders, evangelists, church congregations, as you read this book, which explodes with emotion, take time to understand the importance of 'family.' After one's relationship with the Heavenly Father, souls delivered from demons, the sick healed, and the mentorship of young men and women, what is left? Let me end with this endorsement and sentiment from Anna's dad before he died, [If I had to do it all over again, I would spend more time with you guys. Family is the most important thing in this world.]

"For whosoever shall do the will of my Father which is in Heaven, the same is my brother and sister and mother." Matt. 12:5.

HISTORICAL AND CULTURAL SETTING

This book is very interesting because of the cultural and religious diversity of the nation, from which the writer grew up. It is a nation with a diverse population of varied backgrounds and beliefs, it's political and historical environment stemming from very strong 'east meets west' religions and cultures. From original settlers, French colonization and influences, British protectorate status and the discovery of the island by Spain, brought with it influences of food, religion and a now unique melting-pot culture.

West African slaves, East Indian indentured laborers, their particular beliefs and value systems concerning family ties and human development remained sacrosanct. Established religions were Roman Catholicism, Protestantism under The Church of England, West

African religious practices as the Orisha and The Shouter Baptist, the Evangelicals namely Presbyterians and Methodists and later the Muslims and Hindus. The elders of the aforementioned religions took severe disciplinary measures, and largely felt their children, raised **in strict** culture and religious beliefs, will now "break away" into mixed relationships and nonconformist, non-fundamental religions. The early fifties saw the invasion and excitement of the Pentecostal Movement. The birthing of this "Fire Power Religion" ushered the conversion of many young men and women, to this newfound faith. Ministers enforced a strong disciplined home life, regarding the raising of children, education, marriage and social behavior. Young ministers while pioneering churches and working at secular jobs, felt very strongly the need to raise their children in the niche of 'total obedience'. Pastors' children were subject to intense public scrutiny, therefore behaviors, dress code and the culture of 'do's' and 'don'ts', resulted in severe parental disciplines. Ministers felt they were doing 'right' and strict parenting would ensure that their reputation in the ecclesiastical world would be untarnished. Later, many a family had to sit back in retrospect, watching their children break away, by immigrating to different countries, and making heart-breaking decisions in order to initiate their individuality and talents. Some say glibly, they are the **"Lost Generation".** No! Amidst the harsh criticisms and condemnation, these children now have found what their parents and grandparents **should have taken the time, to invest in them.** Working feverishly to convert and nurture many into becoming well-rounded individuals, they forgot their own and took for granted, that their own-"should know better".

> Dear reader, many preachers' children are still crying out trying to find their way to their destiny and in so doing, eventually find themselves; and purpose for being. I believe, *"The Road Less Traveled"* brings a wake-up call to the clergy and their followers. Instead of 'how will it look' why not pray, counsel, guide gently, teach and show love and understanding.
> *"The foundation of God standeth sure, having this seal, the Lord knoweth them that are His" (II Tim. 2:19).*
> Pastor Selma-Anna's Mom

INTRODUCTION

There seems to be some confusion between being a man's daughter and being the 'Daughter of a Preacher Man'. Life-roles become muddled and sometimes comically confusing. Living on a small island also means living within the confines of small communities with all the gossip, speculation, and parishioners who think they're all entitled to have a 'say' in your life. Just as gossip is typical among people of small towns in parts of America, similar social dynamics are present on small islands where everyone knows everyone else. This social behavior unavoidably creeps into church congregations with far-reaching consequences, under the subtle guise of being one's 'brother's keeper.'

I hope this reflection, though brutally honest, provides insight to the conflicts that face the children of ministers, pastors, religious clergy, deacons, and church leaders. I challenge fellow Christians, to nurture the lives of these children, their gifting and various callings, whatever they may be. I trust this work provokes congregants and leaders to encourage preachers' kids, with tender words, gentle heartfelt guidance and vigilant prayer. I pray this booklet inspires prayer-warriors, to guard over the hearts of the upcoming generation, with loving kindness rather than malicious and piercing words of gossip. As you read this, I hope it would move you toward self-examination and self-correction.

I am a survivor of manmade doctrines and narrow-minded Christian people. I have been battle-scarred and my faith tainted (for a season), by mature folk who metered out judgments and ridicule, enforced dress codes and damned my soul to hell because I began asserting my independence during my teenage years. They felt this behavior was rebellious and unholy and proceeded to sway my father into their way of thinking. Today, I walk as a redeemed soul continually healing in the Light of God's love. Many hurts are healing, battle scars are fading and my King, reinstated to His rightful place, in my heart. Now that I can look forward, I have decided though God's strength, to declare violence against the sins that come against my brothers and sisters in Christ. After all, *[the kingdom suffers violence . . . and this book is about the violent taking it back by force] Matthew 11:12*. At the risk of being politically incorrect, I write these words to grab preachers' kids by force from eternal death, for they too, matter. I have decided to shed light on the emotional and spiritual experiences that I feel, profoundly affect preachers' kids. I hope this provides greater clarity, empathy and patience among God's children. What I offer clergy and peers is hindsight, and my years of experience, as the *'daughter of a preacher man'*.

To protect those I love I have altered names. I have directly quoted passages and paraphrased scripture verses from the Bible using varied versions. I have quoted small parts of well-known songs, paraphrased a statement from one of Rick Joyner's books and referenced Bill Johnson's book Face to Face with God. I have also referenced other writings, books, song lyrics and book titles. If one preacher's kid decides to hold on to Jesus along the way, then sharing these strange life experiences, would have been worth documenting and this journey worth walking.

Here is my disclaimer. I do not have a license in counseling, nor do I have a degree in psychology or theology. I am not an elder or deacon in any church, nor do I hold office as a board member on any religious organization. I am not a minister, pastor or evangelist. I am neither an acclaimed author nor an authority of any kind. Forgive me if I have misquoted scripture or taken verses out of context as this is not my intent. However, I hope the Bible verses I have quoted throughout this booklet would not seem preachy; but then again, I am a preacher's daughter. I trust that these scriptures will grab at your hearts and soothe your soul-wounds. I hope they will provide a new perspective and they would be as you though you are reading them for the first time. I suggest you use the scriptures as a measuring stick by which you judge all statements I have made in this booklet.

I have written this booklet from a different perspective. I am the voice of a group that is easily misunderstood and even shunned. We are the group that, 'should know better.' *'Trust'* is hard to find and 'true friendships' are a priceless novelty. We fiercely guard our loved ones and matters of the heart from you, the outsiders, who can knowingly or unknowingly, inflict deep hurts and severe betrayal. We tend to be a recluse and rebellious bunch because we bear heavy burdens and carry deep battle scars from childhood. We cannot go to anyone with problems and family conflicts, as we are to be beacons of light and hope to other families, the shining examples, so to speak. People expect us to be perfect little robots, dutifully performing our role as 'good preachers' kids,' which I became in public. Organizational church leadership does not tolerate family turmoil and easily meters out quick, efficient judgments and directives, instead of counsel and loving intervention. Just being born into the subculture of 'preachers' kids' we are automatically judged by all, the righteous and the unrighteous alike. We are 'expected to . . .' by default; be good, be upright, make no mistakes, be all things to all men all of the time. We are to be mature in all judgments from the moment of birth, and on and on it goes. I hope these accounts bring insight into our lives, clearing up misgivings and dissipating questions, confusion and fear regarding our behaviors. It is easy for the outsider to criticize, as he or she is not compelled to travel down our path; and few can comprehend our journey toward The Father, *'on a road less traveled'*.

CHAPTER ONE

CHAPTER ONE

MIXED UP YEARS

As a little girl, I was always introverted and a loner yet I was surrounded by Faith, religion and people. Yes, there were lots and lots of people and visitors. There were people with problems, thankful people, well-meaning, loving people and people who stopped off and stayed a while, an unexpectedly **LONG** while. There were girls needing temporary food and shelter because they ran away from their homes, so our home also became a boarding house. They would become very comfortable displacing us girls from our little beds, enjoy our food and home as though entitled. They thought by virtue of being in our home, they were to be my best friend, with exclusive rights to my private thoughts and intimate family confidences. While all this frustration was welling up inside of me, people constantly visited my parents as if our home was a counseling center and it really was. They were unaware and did not truly care whether they intruded on our private family time. There were very few times when dad could sit on the back porch and relax in casual home attire, as we always had some church member living with us. The weather was always hot and sultry and dad would look forward to undressing from formal attire and get into a cool pair of shorts and a sleeveless shirt. Poor guy he could not catch a break and just relax in his favorite pair of 'falling down shorts,' let me explain. My dad was about five feet, two inches tall. He had a small built with a paunch. Over the years, he developed abdominal pains, which became increasingly worse whenever he wore pants that would fit snugly around the waist. My dad often wore pants too big for his physique with belts, so that he could manipulate the tightness or slackness of the waistband. He always looked cute and funny. The following scenario became the daily standing family joke. Mom would often warn dad that his pants would one day, fall down to his knees while walking down the paved pathway to get into the car. He would turn back to glance at her, give her a smirk, pull up his pants and walk down the pathway, with a carefree stride, typical of a young boy kicking pebbles. Guess what, it really happened one day many years later. While dad was walking down that same paved pathway to his car mom warned, he chuckled and walked away as we all stood by happily watching them. Sure enough, the pants slid down to his knees and we all wailed with laughter, and verbal heckles. He too burst out laughing, pulled up his pants with all the dignity he could muster and left for work. Our riotous laughter followed him all the way to the car. Whenever he could, he would sit out on our little back porch on the built-in cemented bench, painted red. My cousin reminded me of her picture of him. He would often be in a white sleeveless, cotton jersey shirt and white shorts at home, which were always too big. While relaxing people would call out at the gate, with a pleading 'Pastor Winston' open the gate and walk right in before anyone had a chance to greet them at the point of entry. These interruptions would always occur and poor dad would jump up out of the seat, hold on to his pants for dear life and run inside to put on long pants and a shirt with sleeves. His deep-seated code of ethics and ministerial protocol never allowed him to present himself to the public, without being appropriately dressed and covered. So that is the story of the 'falling down pants'.

People came at all hours of the day and night needing help. You name the problem our home saw it. Even the demon possessed came to have their souls exorcised at our home. One man even jumped off our two story 'back step' banister-better believe that one! It is no wonder he did not become severely disabled or die as he landed in grandpa's gardening tool shed with pitchforks, rakes, shovels and other sharp tools, which was only covered by a thin sheet of corrugated tin, used for roofing. Go figure! Thank the Lord our neighbor witnessed this crazy act. This was an average day for our family of ministers, so demon-possessed or not, we had ourselves a good laugh after the initial shock of witnessing this act. If you did not laugh, the 'bizarre' and the 'needy' could have easily caused us kids psychological trauma and depression. My dad worked for the municipal government as a clerk, so his salary was adequate. With four kids and one on the way (at that time), we lived modestly. Despite our humble means, dad and mom literally fed and clothed many people and even let them sleep in our beds, while I had to bunk with my sister on her little single bed. She recently reminded me that the bed was so narrow we would have to sleep in alternating positions. Picture this, on hot steamy nights we would have to share my sister's narrow single bed. We would be sweaty, muggy and restless which would result in a terrible night's sleep. The worst part was trying to get some sleep when mosquitoes would buzz around us and sting. Those torturous little creatures were attracted to perspiration and sweaty little girls. During those years, there were no fans to keep us cool and relieve us from the heat. One of us would sleep against the headboard and the other against the footboard so we could both fit. We called it 'head to foot.' The girls who came to live with us often had a bed of their own and the comfort to spread out. We helped many people! Some were never grateful and never looked back with a word of thanks, now that's ministry at personal cost to oneself and one's family. I wonder if that happens today. It seems ministry has changed, since my youthful days. There seems to be more entitlement among new pastors to inherit a mega church. Personal cost and sacrifice such as laying down one's life, is not so popular among today's ministers. My parents literally gave of themselves and paid a high personal price with absolutely no financial or material gain. Many times the people who benefitted the most from my parents' generosity eventually discredited my parents along the way, how pathetic and sad for them.

In retrospect, dad and mom were 'giving' people, oh yes my friends they are 'people' as well as ministers. They were constantly investing in others. They spent many nights counseling families, molding young future leaders and ministers as well as promoting literacy. Their ministry was in the rural unsophisticated Hindu communities of the nation. They sacrificed us all to ensure church members received responsible leadership and Christ-like guidance. Family sacrifice was the order of the day, no questions asked. My sisters and I recently reminisced about those late Sunday nights when dad would counsel people until two and three o'clock in the morning. After long Sunday night services, we would watch as families happily left the church building, not even giving a thought of what the night held for their pastors' kids. We knew what to expect. The nights would be long and buggy and our only ventilation, in a hot church building would be the holes in the wall from the decorative brickwork. The church was too poor to pay for an air conditioning system. To be quite honest the community was so poor I do not think there was competent electrical connection or capacity to put in an air conditioning system anyway. We would frequently watch bugs of unimaginable forms, sizes and colors crawl into the church, on to the walls, floors and even the benches. They were gross and scary. I would frequently have to force my sleepy young siblings to move to another pew to avoid the creepy crawlies. We were all young and Danielle and I would sit on the hard wooden benches and lean on each other to support our tired little bodies. We were the older girls. My eldest brother would curl up on a wooden bench and fall fast asleep. On our laps would be our sleeping baby sisters. Mom and dad would lock themselves in the office or prayer room, with some troubled family or distressed soul for hours. Often times there would be no safe running water to wash the baby bottles. Remember we were in the depths of the countryside. The bathrooms were dirty smelly wooden latrines, which we always prayed we did not have to use. When my baby sisters would cry, from hunger, we could only hold them close and rock them to sleep in comfort. We had no baby food or fresh bottles of baby formula to offer our little siblings, during those early morning hours. All we had were dry empty smelly baby bottles that had the trace of milky baby formula hours prior. In the heat of the night, the stench of the milky trace within the bottles was putrid. Getting home even at four o'clock in the morning would be a welcome relief, as we would collapse into our individual beds, if someone else was not in one of them. It would be a luxury to collapse into our own beds and have a few short hours of restful night's sleep.

Like all other children, we too would have to be up and dressed for school by seven-thirty each Monday morning. We would go to school in a state of exhaustion but this lifestyle was our norm. Dad too would be up before seven in the morning and ready for work all bright eyed and bushy tailed. Mom would often have hot homemade breakfast ready for the family before seven o'clock on a Monday morning. Freshly baked muffins, pancakes, waffles, pastries, Savory eggs and vegetable 'chokas' (sautéed vegetables) with 'roti' (pita bread), would be magically on the table for us all to enjoy, before heading off to school. Dad expected nothing less from us all and we did it because we knew no other way. Family sacrifice was never too great for my parents and the congregants expected us to comply. They were unaware of our sacrifices, so that our parents could be pastors and parents to them and their families. To this day, they do not know we too were ministering to them; and they happily stayed in their ignorance or denial. We were their unpaid worship leaders, choir directors, youth leaders, musicians and outreach team visitors to their humble mud huts. Maybe they did know this but just expected it to be part of the 'pastor's package deal.' Despite the forced service, these experiences taught us to be thankful for our blessings and gave us a strong dose of humility. It taught us how to be *[content in whatever state we were in Phil. 4:11]*. We also knew how to be *'abased'* and how to *'abound' Phil 4:12.* These lessons have followed us throughout our lives and that is why we can be versatile in whatever ministry, job placement or situation we each find ourselves.

Funny thing, my dad always worked a full-time secular job while simultaneously administering the church as a full-time minister with a part-time minister's salary. This was not an issue for him and ministry came from his heart. He loved the flock and cared for them with integrity and honesty. I do not know how the man did it and he will have my eternal respect. Coming to think of it, at age thirty-nine years old, I could barely cope with my full-time job, one graduate class and a baby. Actually every member of my family who was and is in ministry today, have secular jobs and are committed to full-time ministry. Impressively my dad put himself through university in his fifties, as he did not have the opportunity to attend school when he was a young boy. He did this while keeping the congregation going with good leadership and training. He unwaveringly continued his duties on the national Board of Directors of the church organization, to which he belonged. To this day, I cannot imagine how my parents managed to maintain a marriage of forty-something years, (which was not always blissful but stood throughout their years together), multiple pregnancies, the death of a two-day old baby girl, family time, and many ministerial and social obligations, with national and international impact. The amazing thing is both their ministries have managed to alter many lives with far-reaching global and spiritual effects. How did they keep it all together? God alone knows and I do mean that literally.

While we were discussing this booklet, my younger sister Danielle reminded me of further family sacrifices forced upon us. For instance, we frequently stayed at home with my grandparents, which really was a joke. Our home was a two-story, multi-family house in which my grandparents, my aunt, uncle, cousin and I lived upstairs. My dad, mom and siblings lived downstairs. When my parents would leave for meetings, the kids would all stay downstairs so it would be easy for them to get straight into bed. My grandfather would occasionally pop in, as his beloved library was on the first floor. After washing up the dinner dishes, my grandmother would walk down the 'back steps' and also check up on us before retiring upstairs to bed. For the majority of the time we were on our own. This was their idea of supervision, of which we took full advantage. The older ones would really take care of the younger ones and this was no easy task. I was about twelve years old when this babysitting fiasco started and it was a virtually impossible ordeal. No one respected anyone else so there were frequent fights and yelling. Everyone questioned my brother's and my authority and the younger ones often questioned, 'Who put you in charge? You're not the boss of me!' These would be times to be boisterous, obnoxious and out of control. It often resulted in the ruin of mom's high-heeled shoes as we attempted to walk in mom's shoes, so to speak. We would imitate walking as mom did, while she preached her sermons, or practice walking the pretend catwalk, and even dancing in the disco with curtains over the lampshade. Twisted heels were frequently one of the casualties of these frequent crazy nights. Even the few pieces of beautiful china and crystal my mom acquired on her wedding day, did not escape our little destructive hands. Many pieces underwent chips and breakage, as 'playing house' required 'real' dishes of course. There was a lot of 'crying, wailing and gnashing of teeth . . .' to coin a Biblical phrase. Someone always got physically hurt because of someone else's antics. What would one expect, when children age twelve and under were left on their own?

I could vividly remember my brother Brandon, roughly playing with one of my younger sisters, Natasha, who was already hurt in a prior car accident with stiches on her head. I warned him that she could hit her head and the stitches could open up. Well, he placed her in a cardboard box to simulate a car. Yes, I am sure you see it coming. The box capsized and down went Natasha face first. Her head hit the edge of mom's wooden shoe stand and phew, BLOOD SPILLED! I am sure the Lord was empathetic that night to the spillage of blood that occurred and the pain we all had to endure from (what is known in my country as), 'a good cut tail.' The wound burst open and her forehead bled profusely! Someone took her to the hospital either my grandparents or my uncle and aunt who lived upstairs; and we all received beatings and punishment that we will never forget as long as we are alive! Yes folks this was a typical night on our own while mom and dad were out saving souls and ministering to the lost. We all helped each other with schoolwork and relied on each other while mom and dad were out of the house, even though my grandparents were upstairs and around. I would often prepare dinner for the younger ones and get them ready for bed, before beginning my homework around ten o'clock at night or even later. All we had to hold on to was each other because our parents were constantly out on the battlefield. They left us so they could bring you the lost sheep to Jesus. My sister Roz even thought at times, I was her mom because I would often take care of her and put her to bed while she twirled her fingers in my hair, until she fell asleep. She was my little live doll as we had a thirteen-year difference. I felt mom and dad had her just for me. My own little sister-daughter, she fulfilled my desire to love a little one and take care of that little soul. She was going to feel special all the days of her life, I would see to that. It was a feeling we lacked each time we would congregate on the porch and watch our parents drive away from us and toward the lost. I made sure she would never feel insecure and invisible. She was mine to love, to spoil rotten and I was going to make sure she felt like the world's most beautiful princess. I made sure she would not feel as though she was part of an invisible package, expected to serve dutifully. I ensured that she knew she was here because we wanted her. I let her know she was here for us to love her, to grow in beauty and grace, to love life with abandonment and joy. Guess what, she is still full of life and beauty. She loves the Lord and now willingly serves with my mom in the administration of the ministry with little financial payment. She serves the brethren without a sense of obligation or coercion. She serves the Bride out of the desire of her heart and in the freedom of God's love.

Going back to that time I remember that my dad always managed to feed and clothe us in a decent manner. Guess my parents struggled for money and we were not aware of it. I could recall a funny story well in retrospect it is funny now. There was a time when my mom bought three bolts of dress material a bolt has yards of material. There was a seamstress in the church, who offered to sew some dresses for us. Guess mom thought it was a great money-saving idea at the time. Well it turned out to be quite a fiasco at least in my mind any way. Need I say that the seamstress, in all her creativity, had sewn all three sets of dresses in the same style and in the same fabric for all three girls! She did not even think of using each bolt of material to create three different styles of dress for each girl. I just cannot forget sister Janice for that one. It did not help that I was an adolescent at the time, and I would have to attend church wearing the same dress as my sisters! Turned out my two sisters would be dressed just like me and we would be in church together looking like, 'Sisterly Sisters', a very sarcastic disdainful term I would say to them, to dissuade them from wearing the same dress I was wearing. My sister Danielle would deliberately provoke me by wearing the same thing I wore, or at least that was how I interpreted her behavior. In hindsight, she just wanted to feel like a 'big girl' and have the security of belonging. She was really looking up to me and wanted to identify with me, her big sister. Of course, I was too self-absorbed, humiliated and immature to perceive this. It was just painful and embarrassing, although now humorous in hindsight. Each time I wore the same dress as my sisters, I felt as though the world was ending or at least it should have. As you can tell, the world did not end and I survived this excruciating and public coming-of-age issue. Need I say I fought with my siblings every week if they chose to wear the same dress as I did, boy would we fight! Talk about "warfare" and this would be before even getting into the car for church. *I thought I should share this humorous memory, to add to my identity crisis at the time.*

We would take these heated verbal feuds straight into the car and on the way to services. Despite our weekly disruptive, loud and obnoxious behaviors in the car, dad was able to tune us out and practice his homiletically correct sermon, before arriving at church. Could you believe he was able to tune us all out, I still do not know how he did that! Unbelievably, the man was a genius at compartmentalizing and focusing on a task! By the time we would get to church, we already heard the entire sermon of choice. Yet, when dad delivered each sermon from behind the pulpit, the impact was great, as though we never heard the sermon before that moment. It was always the Holy Spirit ministering to our little hearts. We all had our favorite sermons and to this day, each of us could quote parts of them verbatim.

Now here is a little fox in the newly blossoming vineyard, so to speak. My mom, also a minister, just loves people. It is just her thing. So get this, much to my irritation everyone was introduced us as "aunt this" or an "uncle that". It was very intrusive, to be obligated to call strangers by such an intimate title, as they were not part of my family, nor were they welcome in our tightly closed circle. I was very resentful about that as you can well imagine, and much preferred to call these persons 'mister . . . .' or 'misses . . .' or nothing at all. I would say things, like 'hello, how are you? That was how I escaped referencing people by any family titles. Why did mom give them the liberty to think they were part of my precious family, I just do not understand. Addressing someone by 'uncle' or 'aunt' was an intimate respectful endearment with connotations of trust, family love and security. I felt none of those things towards these strangers. Unfortunately, my mom unknowingly, pushed these people on us all. I would continually feel as though they were squeezing life out of me and I could not breathe. People constantly smothered me and to this day, I avoid crowds. Soon these strangers thought it was their God-given duty to share their unwanted advice with us, regarding behavior, clothing, wearing make-up (Jezebel behavior), dating, education and everything else you could possibly think of. I remember how church members criticized my little sisters because they began wearing mismatched stockings, wearing a bunch of bangles or colorful silly bands on their arms and combing their ponytails on one side of their heads. Well before long, they were considered ungodly, bad influences and going to hell. The church folk did not forget me either as I was now the devil's child when I first wore eyeliner and lip-gloss at the age of seventeen. How could they forget, I was supposed to be their gift from God, as I was the one who 'blessed them in song' each week. These so-called Christians were fickle, religious and judgmental! Now, why would adults be concerned with someone else's child's coming of age, why I ask! Do you see the light? Early intrusions though they seemed well-meaning began invading our early blossoming years. It reminds me of a passage from the wise King Solomon, *"Take us the foxes, the little foxes that spoil the vineyards; for our vineyards are in blossom" Song of Solomon 2:15.*

While growing up, we were confined by ultra-strict traditional standards and organizational church rules, some good, some tiresome. Dress codes were rigidly enforced and the presence of our company was mandatory at every single service, by parents and church members alike. We could not wear long or short pants, as this piece of clothing was 'men's apparel' as dictated by the missionaries-try learning to ride a bicycle in a skirt or hang upside down from my uncle's swing. Television was a curse of the devil infiltrating the homes and minds of us youth, in retrospect there is some truth to this. At the time though, Brady Bunch and The Electric Company, made this perception seem extreme. Teenage crushes were not typical innocent growth and development but giving in to 'passion' and 'fleshly desires.' Give me a break-as though I even knew what that meant! My family always redirected boys in the opposite direction from us girls, as they were a 'threat to a girl's virginity.' Who was thinking about that at age twelve, could you believe that craziness! After those over-reactions, I made it my business to find out all I could about boys, as I got older. It was at this point that, the initial seed of rebellion became rooted into my life just because people got in the way. Over the years however, my dad and mom became more realistic and we developed some awesome friendships with the opposite sex that still last today. As the family grew in size, my parents became less rigid. They developed unique parenting styles that were appropriate, flexible and effective for each child's personality. They eventually learned how to love and enjoy their children. They stopped succumbing to the dictates of others, on 'how to parent' their kids. My dad learned how to celebrate our humanity, our personalities, our wit, our uniqueness, and our achievements. He even acknowledged our insecurities and doubts without judgment or criticism and waited for us all, to work out our own salvation so to speak.

To this day, the effects of the 'little foxes' have left me an introvert and untrusting of others. I value my privacy and the privacy of my family and my home. This attitude was eventually the open stairway to my spiritual downward spiral, which would occur within a few short years. Not many understand why I have few friends, less than two fingers on one hand, and I am pretty much "people phobic as well as crowd phobic." I am the first to admit these are not phobias to have, if one has to reach souls for the Kingdom. To be honest, when I meet people who talk too much I just tune them out. I immediately begin seeing them transform into two gigantic lips, standing in front of me saying a lot of nothingness, 'flapsin' as my grandmother would put it. It is, as the Bible describes, no love and no substance, just annoying *'sounding brass'* and irritatingly *'clanging cymbals'* 1 Cor. 13:1. These harsh realities are cruel and ungracious to say to the people of God but good Christian folk inflicted these life-impacting scars with their invasion of thoughtlessness and insensitivity. My grandmother always said to us, 'words have life'. Bottom line is my reaction of becoming people-phobic, is the outcome of peoples' words and intrusive verbal behaviors at a young age. I was too immature to process the 'people invasion.'

Unfortunately, these behaviors left me so guarded in life they have intruded into my adulthood and stunted my spiritual growth for many years. I have literally sat back and done nothing as humanity journeys away from the Savior. I am in the process of mending and healing, and it is ongoing until Jesus comes. This is just an example of how these intrusive "little foxes" have unfortunately crippled my ministry, up until now. My husband cannot understand my automatic aversion to talkative people, who presumptuously and immediately familiarize themselves with my family and me. I instantly hear myself automatically tell my husband statements like, 'that person is like a pair of big 'flapsin' lips. What did that person say, I wasn't listening,' as I tune them out. I am sure my peers out there understand. This unfortunately has been my harsh reality for years and these little intrusions have caused me to develop into a tough and cold person, until now. Guess it is one of my scars not quite completely healed but God's love is making, '. . . old things pass away and all things new' 2Cor. 5:17.

Since this realization, I have been allowing Jesus and Holy Spirit to cause my soul to line up with the spirit man. I am becoming less reactive to people and their sins. Each day I sanctify myself with the washing of the Word so that the fruits of His Spirit like gentleness, meekness and temperance are the good works He completes within me. Like the apostle, *[I don't understand myself at all . . . and my bad conscience proves that I agree with these laws I am breaking . . . I am no longer doing it. It is sin inside me that is stronger than I am that makes me do these evil things. It seems to be a fact of life that when I want to do what is right, I inevitably do what is wrong. When I want to do good, I don't; and when I try not to do wrong, I do it anyway . . . In my mind I want to be God's willing servant but instead I find myself still enslaved to sin . . . my new life tells me to do right, but the old nature that is still inside me loves to sin. Oh, what a terrible predicament I'm in! Who will free me from my slavery to this deadly lower nature? Thank God! It has been done by Jesus Christ our Lord. He has set me free.] Ro. 7:15-25 (Life Application Bible The Living Bible).* For many years I have had to minister to myself in psalms as I tried in myself to do those things that are right and kept failing because I did them in my own strength. This was my psalm, for a long time, which I wrote many years ago.

How many times have I made up my mind not to fail You
How many times have I said, I'll go on strong.

How many times have I told all the world, I love You
Then turned my back on your love and walked right out.

CHS:
Lord you never, you never turn your back on me
You never see the failures I see
You're my strength Lord, when I become too weak.
Lord you never, you never turn your back on me

How many times in my living, I crucify you
How many times will you say, I forgive
How many times will take, my broken promises
And tenderly say to me, child I know you'll win.

People out there:

I have a tip for some of you well-meaning people. Do not go up to a preacher's kid and start sermonizing with scripture and verse or begin giving unwanted advice. It is just that, **unwanted advice.** Guess what, we know all those scriptures and we can even put a spin on them that can send you into shock, just to get a good laugh. I do apologize for my candid words but I really cannot tolerate meaningless chatter and probably so do most of the preachers' kids out there. Like you, we too have to *[work out our own salvation . . .] Ph. 2:12.*

Pastors are stewards to nurture the sheep. You are the sheep. We are their children, their family. We respect you and your families, the hours of stewardship required and we honor our parents' commitment. However, please let our parents, parent us. They are our parents first. We are constantly under their spiritual guidance and counsel so they know what is best for us. Thank you very much for your support but they can parent us very well without intrusive advice and mentorship. To all the *'We know what's better for you than your parents'* type of people. **Us preachers' kids (PKs) do not need many parents, just our own, thank you very much. Dad and mom could handle it!**

We all need to experience salvation. *[We are born in sin and shaped in iniquity. Ps.51:5]* Do not forget, in a child's coming of age he or she is in the *process* of discovering and experiencing salvation. Your actions and reactions to them during this time are critical.

You could be a safe haven for these children or acts of stoning and condemnation. My fellow Christians don't forget, *"there is therefore now no condemnation to them which are in Christ . . . they that are after the flesh mind the things of the flesh; but they that are after the Spirit the things of the Spirit" Ro. 8:1&5.* Encourage these children to take their place in ministry. Pray for their salvation and steadfastness in the Lord. While finding their way they may stumble and fall, so you may want to pray for them unceasingly. Encourage them by showing love and kindness. Leave judgment to the Perfect Judge. A simple smile or just being quiet and tolerant through their awkward stages will minister to many preachers' kids. It can mean the difference in children turning away from Jesus out of despair or grabbing hold to Truth and Light. Pray for these kids in Love as they are constantly under the attack of the enemy. That is why *". . . the greatest of these is Love" 1Cor. 13:13.*

Parents of Preacher's Kids (PK's):

You need to believe in your stewardship to your babies. They are just that, yours to care for lovingly and gently. My dad always opened his arms as big as he could, call us all to him and say*, [Happy is the man whose quiver is full . . .] Ps. 127:5. [My children are olive plants around my table] Ps. 128:3.* He would smile and hug us. For a split moment in time, it would make this crazy world of ours seem perfect. It is okay to consume your family with love; and have their love consume you. God wants you to enjoy your family boundlessly. Then you can say what my dad used to say, like David the psalmist, *[happy am I and it is well with me] Ps. 128:2.* I remember he would say these words at the table each time he surveyed his family during a meal. Throughout the years, dad continually proclaimed these words and to this day, they bring me great joy and validation. Writing this, puts a tickle in my stomach, a childlike joy in my heart and a huge smile on my face. Take time to minister to your children, as it will give them much joy and peace into adulthood. Parental love is so important to Jesus, he has aligned one of his roles and relationships to humankind, to that of a parent. He has reassured us that he will be a *'A father to the fatherless . . .' Ps. 68:5* Parental love and guidance is not a relationship to take for granted. This is your validation from the Heavenly Father that it is okay to embrace your babies wholly. His love personifies, symbolizes and reinforces parent-child love. God our Father and Jesus His Son are wonderful examples of love, the love that should define all family relationships. Protect and cocoon your parent-child love from outside influences.

Preachers' Kids (PK's):

Take care not to mind the little foxes. Do not let them creep in and get ahold of your soul as bitterness can easily set in, and cause an entrance into an abyss of spiritual disconnect. Hold on tightly to Jesus and your relationship with Him. Your spirit man is whole and perfected in Jesus' ultimate love sacrifice on the cross. You *are* a new person in Christ. However, take care of your soul man, your mind, as this is the place where foxes penetrate. So, remember *[He will keep you in perfect peace whose mind is stayed (focused) on Him because you trust in the Lord.] Is. 26:3.*

CHAPTER TWO

STEALING AWAY

Every day after getting home from school, I would run away to my cousin's homemade swing in her back yard. I would spend all day at school, thinking of those moments when I could get out of my brown and white uniform and start swinging, after a long hot day. Thank God for Uncle Evan! Wow, he was so '**normal**'. He put together this silver steel frame, which still stands today. The swing had fat silver chain links that went all the way up from the thick red-painted wooden seat to the steel frame. The steel and sliver would glisten in the sun like a beautiful gleaming edifice, catching my eye, while walking home from school each day. It stood there beckoning me for heavy-duty swinging action. Its structure stood mighty and strong with sturdy cross bars ready for tumbling, climbing and summersaulting children, never weakening under the demanding pressure of my many siblings and cousins. Its tall shiny stance dared us to escape to worlds of freedom, wondrous dreams and delightful hours of imagination. To this day, I can say out of all the physical things in this world, I love that swing the best! It was my strong quiet companion and it held my dreams and heart's desires and kept many secrets without betrayal or opinion. My uncle Evan truly is a God-sent. He made the 'great escape' just for me and did not even know it. I consider myself a 'swing' expert and I have yet to see a swing that can compare to 'Mighty and Strong.' Yes, I know it is fruity but I named the swing in my head.

My uncle Evan could also get a great chuckle out of every family member's "humanness". The chuckle was invaluable, as all the adults in my household were ministers with a holy standing, who walked the rigid straight and narrow, a little wearisome for us young folk back then. He gave me an escape 'far from the maddening crowd' (to use Thomas Hardy's book title 1874), by building that awesome swing. I would swing as high as I could possibly go, at times almost falling out of the swing. On a hot tropical island, the swing is a terrific cooling device. Its natural movement and inertia could induce short bursts of breezes and cooling winds, on a hot, dry day. This was true freedom. My hair would be loose from its constrained ponytail at the end of the day and the rush of breezes would flow through my hair at the force of the swing's propulsion. I was in control when I was on that swing. I could control and create a wind. What fun, what power, and no boundaries of any kind. I felt I could supersede gravity and in my mind, I did. There were no people to talk to, no spiritual intrusions, no disdainful homework, and no expectations. I would no longer be claustrophobic by the intrusion of people. I would be free to breathe, to think, to move, to laugh out loudly, and to shout if I felt like it. My universe came alive when I was on that swing as my mind would explode with imagination and creativity, bottled up inside because the world demanded that I stay focused on schoolwork, household chores and church obligations. I did not even have to mind my manners when I was soaring through the air at the speed I chose. I loved the control within this quiet and peaceful environment. I was blank and had the joy of enveloping nature and seeing where it would take my mind and imagination. In a few hours of swinging, I could be a model, a hot pop singer, a mom with a strong handsome husband, a teacher or explore the sky, the stars and outer space. I could sometimes get a very clear picture in my mind of Heaven as described in the Bible. The warm air was always fragrant with the smell of the earth and tropical flowers of all kinds, as my aunt and uncle planted flowers, throughout the big rolling grassy front yard. Some days I could smell the newly cut grass and I would inhale deeply. These moments tickled me deep inside right down to my toes.

I would sing all the songs Gramps would sing for me every night. Amidst all this holiness I would belt out 'In my little red boat', 'How would you like to go up in a swing', 'Move all your Fingers', those were the good innocent ones. Then, my favorite repertoire of songs would follow. Songs I chose to sing of my own free will . . . 'Fernando', 'Let Me Be There', 'I'm On The Top Of The World . . .,' 'I Honestly Love You', 'Tennessee Waltz', 'The Closer I Get to you' and many, many more unholy pop songs, too many to mention. Wow, I could sing. I had a strong, clear beautiful voice at that time. 'Oh no, I would think, I like songs from the radio that has nothing to do with church and God'. Am I going to hell, I wondered. I ask you, should a poor little girl be tormenting herself with such nonsense, but I did.

Every day I would sing my repertoire of 'ungodly' songs and steal away into a world of imagination. The audience was not a congregation but rowdy, young people clamoring for me to come on stage and perform songs about real life and real feelings, not insinuating for a minute that Christianity is not real. At that time, my cousin Rebecca and my beloved uncle Evan were the only ones who knew how much

I loved Roberta Flack, Diana Ross, Abba, Olivia Newton-John, Anne Murray, The Carpenters, Kenny Rogers and Marvin Gaye, just to name a few pop artists. Every evening my cousin Rebecca and I would escape down to the first floor of her house and blast the records. We would sing and dance with full out choreography too, oh yes we did! I am so dating myself, as there are no such things as records anymore just mp3's and iTunes, I'm so obsolete. She and I were the same age and we clung to each other for friendship, love and emotional support. We had a trust between us like sisters. I would often think to myself, 'Oh no, I am partaking in worldly music and I am going straight to hell in a hand basket that I am weaving every day!' Why should I experience so much confusion and mixed feelings by enjoying great love songs? Yet I could not stop. To compensate for my 'carnal nature' I would be a good little girl, listen to everyone, try to abide by the Ten Commandments, very hard especially when I was 'cheating' and 'lying' by indulging in worldly music with unbridled passion.

Gramps was a wonderful literary scholar in the nation and a spiritual leading giant with a quiet and humble disposition. He instilled in me the love for poetry, prose and song. His literary work exclusively reflected his love for Jesus and God's goodness. As he gave me more and more I was feeling guilty that I was writing lyrics for 'the devil'. I was deeply guilt-ridden but that did not stop my love for worldly pop music and lyrics. I would go to school and daydream in class about everything a little girl would daydream about in her little life. I would write love verses, make up rhyming songs and wonder about pretty dresses, having my very own bedroom, having an awesome career in a big city, marriage and BOYS, the devil's ultimate temptation. Need I say, church and God never entered those thoughts and I never let it, as this was *my* time and *my* head, are you starting to see the picture taking shape? By the way, all this was happening between the ages of eight and sixteen. I was just too young to deal with this 'stuff'. Disoriented and confused, these things made me grow up prematurely. Guilt and shame plagued me from the early days of my youth and I was a tortured soul just by being a preacher's kid.

Parents of PK's:

It is okay to have places of escape for your little ones, away from the church and the demands of the people. Give yourselves permission to enjoy alone time, freedom and creativity. Leisure time for your kids and yourself renews and refreshes. One's mind can create and perceive clearer after you allow yourself time to rest. It is quite okay for your kids to draw, dance, sing, twirl, act and just goof off. Allow them to be kids. Escapism and fun is not sin. It is good for them to know they have a place to call their own, a place of quiet restful joy and no intrusions. Play a little and laugh much with your kids. Take a roll down a grassy hill with them and feel pure exhilaration. Even God in all His might, wisdom and glory, rested after all that creative work. He sat back and enjoyed His work calling it 'good.' You too, can sit back and call your work 'good,' put it in its place and enjoy your true inheritance, your kids.

PK's:

It is quite okay to exhale long and hard. Nothing is wrong with finding your private secret place in this huge noisy world, which bombards us daily. Maybe you can find a big old tree in your yard, a boulder to sit on, a gently trickling stream or even the library to call your own. My bed with its fiber filling poking out from the mattress and not very comfortable but was my other secret place, when strangers were not sleeping in it. Despite its discomfort, it was my spot, my familiar safe place to sleep, dream and daydream. I spent hours lying on that bed, with my feet propped on the windowsill, staring up into the sky. I often wished I could float on one of those white fluffy clouds that would fill our island sky. They would be huge and I would wait for the next bunny, airplane or other surprising shape to form. This quieted my heart and mind and I would meditate and think of God and Heaven. I would will Jesus to appear in the sky and wait so quietly I could hear my heartbeat and soft breath sounds. I would hope for the impossible sighting of an angel flitting by or something just as beautiful. I would be in a hushed state of expectancy so as not to scare an angel or even Jesus. I would be in awe of creation and compare myself to the grand universe. I would wonder how Jesus saw me. I guess I was praising, worshiping and meditating on His goodness, his handiwork and his omnipotence. I did not even realize it, as these moments in time did not involve a format, a protocol, a time limitation or pronouncements of any kind. It was just a sweet communion with daddy God. I was a child of wonder and yearning for my supernatural Heavenly Father. I yearned to connect with the Creator of this awesome Universe. These are the times my friends, when your spirit can connect with God's Spirit without interference from people and other noisy distractions. Quietness is good and underrated in a world of continual distractions from people, electronic devices and excessive traffic. In quiet times, you can hear the Spirit say 'come' and you can arise to your glorious, spectacular friend, Jesus. In a world of noise, allow quietness and peace to enter into your hearts and let them reign in daily moments of your lives. You will be amazed, at the revelation that unfolds within your spirit from your Heavenly Father. Here is an example of the outcome of this type of worship.

> You are great, My dear Lord
> You are great, beyond the stars
> Forevermore, beyond time
> You are great, Adonai.

CHAPTER THREE

ON-STAGE PERFOMANCES

When I was eight years old, my family discovered and harnessed my singing talent, especially my grandmother. It started with my cousin Shelly. We were an extended family and I lived upstairs with my grandparents and 'Shelly's' parents. My mom told me she was extremely sick when I was born and my grandmother took care of me. The last of my grandmother's daughters got married and well I took her place. My grandparents adored me and formed such a bond with me I just continued living with them upstairs. That too had some emotional ambiguities but I had more than enough love from all the grandparents, parents, aunts and uncles. My parents continued living downstairs all their married lives. Anyway, Shelly became proficient at playing the piano and began practicing some 'modern, pop-sounding' church songs. I began singing along as she taught me the lyrics to the songs she was playing. I was not aware that the adults were listening when Shelly and I began harmonizing and belting out the songs. To my dismay and pleasure, I found myself on the stage, with a microphone in my hand singing and moving souls nearer to Jesus. How did I get this responsibility, it was baffling. Now I had 'The Gift' and 'The Curse.' The applause and appreciation were wonderful! I also felt as though I was doing something worthwhile even though my heart was yearning to sing a love song, and perform at a live concert. To be honest I did not want the hidden agenda of wooing souls to spiritual conviction, as I had not yet experienced the salvation process. All I knew was that I was 'up there' on stage. God had not yet 'called me', or so I thought. Suddenly, I had to live with the responsibility that my every action was accountable to God, parents and humankind because I was standing as an 'ambassador' for Christ. The magnitude of my responsibility was overwhelming! My family members were easily recognizable because of their years of educational service and spiritual leadership throughout the nation. This meant there was no place to hide. There was no refuge and all of my actions and behaviors were constantly under scrutiny by all types of people. My friends thought I should always give in when we played games because I was the preacher's kid. My headmistress thought I should be a math genius because I was the preacher's kid and from a brilliant family.

To make matters worse my God-fearing grandmother used to irritate me by having me sing to every single person that visited our home.

More irritatingly, she would make me sing a church song whether the persons could appreciate its message or not. I could see the visitors bored to tears not understanding what I was singing about and painstakingly waiting for me to complete my renditions. They listened out of respect for my grandmother. You could see in their eyes and body language, they were tolerating me and they were just waiting for me to complete this forced 'nuisance.' They would politely and condescendingly smile, unable to maintain eye contact due to the awkwardness of the entire fiasco. These experiences never seemed to end, quickly enough. They were humiliating and degrading to me and I wished no one knew I could sing. Could you imagine the torture for a normal little girl who wanted to be just that, 'a little girl'? My grandmother would call me away from my wondrous swing to face these unfamiliar adult strangers and provide karaoke renditions. Somehow my cousin Sherry was either not around or got out of these ordeals, huh, gotta ask her about that.

All of a sudden, this little girl was in the limelight and people constantly pointed their fingers at me. People were judging me all the time and I was under harsh and cruel scrutiny. The church people had not realized that I honed in on my talent and 'blessed' them at every service, by learning songs and singing techniques from the aforementioned pop singers, the worldly people. How ironic is that folks? I sang just about everywhere, in modest little churches, under raised or stilted wooden homes in our rural countryside; spreading the gospel with my uncle and aunt, parents and grandparents. I sang in big churches to hundreds at a time and made appearances in concert halls and large auditoriums. Oh, the power to move masses of people to 'good', and the applause, oh the' applause'! To this day, no experience or accomplishment can compare to 'The Applause' and feeling of stardom. I do not know if I am going to hell for having that thought but this was my thought at the time. Of course, you feel secretly justified because you are really doing a good thing for God and the people. To be quite honest I loved the 'power' of little old me moving the crowd. My clear-pitched voice at that time, allowed me to indulge in my love of song and music. I loved the applause and the adulation and justified it by thinking I was helping lost souls find their way to the true higher Power. Meanwhile it fed into my imaginary world of becoming a worldwide singing sensation and my private little ego trip, sorry honesty is hard to swallow. Time went by and I kept on going, searching, growing, learning and seeking.

At about age twelve, something wonderful and not so wonderful happened. I got a chance to compete in a children's talent show. Here was my out and new beginning I thought, 'the world will see me bust out now.' 'The secret sensation the hidden talent will be revealed' I thought; but true to form, my family did not allow me to blow the competition away with 'Somewhere over the Rainbow' but 'Jesus is the Answer.' I was so disappointed and mad, downright mad! Here was my chance to compete in the real world and this was what I was compelled to sing! What a disappointment! Anyway, I got first prize in the preliminary and lost in the semi finals, with 'A Bright New World'.

Get the picture people, my realistic aunt and uncle allowed my cousin Rebecca to perform a piano recital from Mozart or one of the greats. She went on to the finals. Is something wrong with this picture? It sure is. Not everything is God, or at least that was what I thought back then. To phrase it more appropriately I would say, some things are just within the 'normal' scope of living, which God blesses. I believe this is conquering Kingdom domains within our lifetime. This would fall under the domain of arts and entertainment.

Parents of PKs:

Give it all a break. The kids get it more than you think. They are born into this world, and if you trust in The King and His Word you won't lose any of these little ones, as they are *[not of this world . . . Jo. 17:16]*. They will find Him in their way and through Jesus. Trust in the promises of the Bible. Declaring the Word on their lives, would release the angels to minister to your children. It is okay to love them because they are your kids to love. Be secure in your spiritual parenting. You are only their stewards. They will find personal intimacy with God and experience the King in their own time and only through their own personal experiences. Parents, those Word-filled sermons that you preach every service, do get into the hearts of your kids, and I should know. They stay in our hearts when we walk on the mountaintop close with God, or when we are downtrodden in the pigpens with evil all around. Your sermons echo in our hearts and minds when we are walking through hell on earth or sitting on the fences of indecision. Simply practice what you preach when you deal with these precious ones. There is nothing to gain by imprisoning your kids, with your type of religious convictions and rules. Your kids will always be relevant to their generation *[new wine in new skins . . .] Matt 9:17*. Parents you should know all too well that, when you put old wine in new wine bottles or skins they will break or burst. It is not about what you want for these kids.

Maintain balance and give your kids a chance to experience personal growth and eventual independence. Give them a chance to blossom into unique individuals. *They are relevant to their generation.* The kids are probably more relevant to their generation than you are. Let them discover their own identities and become beautiful Christian persons. Trust in your parenting skills and *[let God complete the work which He has begun] Phil. 1:6*.

It is amazing when I think about it but ministers of the last decade or century would be highly offended to see ministers and congregants wearing jeans and casual clothing to church today. Yet masses are turning to Christ, supernatural miracles are manifesting, and the spirit of Elijah is breaking through, as the church has never seen. Let me draw your attention to yet another example. The music heard worldwide in Christian churches today, is acceptable now and was relevant to my generation when I was growing up but it was not permissible in the church back then. Those songs and rhythms were 'sinful', 'worldly', 'unsanctified' and 'indecent' in churches of yesteryear. We were the ones breaking in 'contemporary Christian music' and not without much criticism, curiosity and mixed reactions from the congregants and ministers.

God gives your children the gifts and He will develop them in His time. Once you are preparing their spirits to be sensitive to the Father's Spirit, He will do the rest. Parents why put your children's Christianity on show before they work out their salvation. Guide your precious ones. There is no need to push them into roles, for which they are not quite ready.

PKs:

Make no mistake kids; there is nothing *'normal'* about you! [***Before the foundation of the earth, God called you and set you apart for His pleasure. Rom.8:29]***. You were preordained to ministry and you are like the descendents of the tribe of Levi, born into ministry and service of the greatest King of all times. He has enlisted you and what a privilege, whatever your ministry may be. You have already been ***chosen by God,*** whether you like it or not You have not just been ***called*** by the King of kings, but you have been ***chosen*** by Him before the foundation of the world *(**Matt. 22:14**).* The Old Testament is a pattern for the New. In ***Exodus30:29-33*** God was specific in the anointing of Aaron and his sons for ministry within the tabernacle. God did not call Aaron and friends but the direct descendants of Aaron. The oil used for the separate anointing of Aaron and his children throughout generations could not be poured on any man's flesh and not be used for anything else but the anointing of the priesthood throughout generations. Their father's ministry and total commitment to ministry was far-reaching throughout all generations. You have the inheritance and supernatural anointing for priesthood, which upon anyone else could be detrimental. God's anointing is set aside specifically for you and your ministry to the world. Wake up it is a serious, powerful and holy anointing from the God of Israel. In other words, the finger of God is on you my comrades. Have yourselves a good long read and know who you are in Christ Jesus. Let that scripture seal your past, your present and your future.

There is a difference between your ***creativity*** and your ***ministry*** my friends. A person's talent is not necessarily his or her ministry although one can compliment the other. Embrace them both but be aware of the defining lines. I have found that my ministry changes and evolves with each season. Sometimes God uses my musical talents to minister to others. At other times, God decides that I need to engage in intercessory prayer for a season. There are times the Creator uses me to comfort the sick and dying just by listening or providing a soothing touch and embrace. At one point in time, God actually used me to preach, yes preach, you heard me, little old me I know, it is unbelievable! It was a small, rural church and I was one of the more spiritually mature persons in the congregation. I did not realize it back then but my exposure to a lifetime of sermons and pastoral leadership prepared me for this period in life. My pastor back then, recognized that I was ready for street evangelism and so God used me to preach.

Your ministry is a diverse unique evolving entity, and relevant to wherever you are in life and to whomever you meet, that is what makes you dynamic. The Holy Spirit gives us gifts of His Spirit, so we can bear His fruit in the right season and in the right time. My comrades *[if we abide in Christ, He abides in us we will have sweet fellowship and become one with Him we can ask at will, and it shall be done. Jo 15:7.] [We will be as trees planted by the rivers of living water. He is our Water of Life sustaining us from our roots and hydrating our system with Life so we can bear His fruit in the right season . . . John 15: 4, 5, and 8].* Our relationship with Christ is as water is to a tree. Once we dig deep into this relationship, (as roots of trees grow deep into the earth and find water), and drink, we will gain Life and be able to share Life with others. Unlike earthly relationships, you get much more than you have invested into your relationship with Christ. The yield is astronomical because the Creator is limitless and unfathomable. You only have to pursue Him to find out.

Whether you know it or not, your exposure to all facets of ministry is in preparation to serve those in need, who you will meet along your journey. *[There is a time and season for everything under the sun Ecc.3:1.]* Someone else may not be able to change hats and be as diversified as you. That is because you have an awesome exposure and training ground. You are experiencing varying strengths, strategies and pitfalls of pastoring a congregation, leading the flock and ministering to the hurt and the needy. You are experiencing varying personalities within the church, so you can be all things to all men. See, there is a reason for this inexplicable road you are traveling. God is preparing you to be relevant and flexible to deal with many different types of people and situations. You may flinch at the word 'ministry' so consider yourself *'relevant'*. God has not allowed me to stagnate. I can tell you this; I have been many things in life and some of them not so good. Nevertheless, in whatever situation I have found myself, I have never been *irrelevant.* Like it or not, I have always been in the right place, at the right time and in the right circumstance to do the King's will, even if the place was dark and foreboding. He has been with me all the time.

When the King of kings begins to make you relevant to others, embrace it wholeheartedly with humility and gusto, with reverence and joy.

You are in the greatest, most powerful plan of your life. You cannot imagine where it will lead you. Why let anyone steal the joy, wonder and adventure of your personal faith in God? Compare a limitless, powerful, miraculous relationship with the Creator of the universe to a relationship with the ultimate liar, limited created being, a perpetual wannabe, counterfeit spirit destined to eternal torture. Anyway, as you explore your creativity and develop your gifting it will eventually turn into 'ministry' or 'relevance' whichever term floats your boat.

Let me explain further, I wrote a song for mentally challenged kids. Someone approached my aunt to write a song for children with disabilities, to increase national awareness. She approached me with the project and I wrote words and music in one day (a few hours actually). I tweaked the song, the following day. My cousins who were born with disabilities were my inspiration and the Holy Spirit, quickly brought words and melody into my head. This I feel, was the bigger picture and one of the reasons for growing up with cousins who have special needs. Their needs facilitated increased national awareness and change for a needy population. I could not keep up with the pace of inspiration. I can say today the entire composition process, was from the 'Big Man Above'. Now that was creativity turning into ministry at the nation's point of need. I gave it to my sister Natasha to sing and record and she gained national notoriety in the media. She broke through to the secular part of our society. It was not a Christian song but Holy Spirit knew the need to increase awareness of this disability and this hurting population. The song attracted executives, noteworthy media personalities and people in high places to be a blessing to this cause. It brought social consciousness to a neglected population in my country through a gospel singer. That is Kingdom ministry! It addressed a social issue from a Spirit-filled perspective. Holy Spirit had a plan for my years of exposure to my cousins with special needs, a grandfather who nurtured the love for writing and poetry skills and a family of musicians. I would call that, ministry. Let me share the words of the song with you so that you can get a clearer understanding of what I mean by God using the song to influence the attitudes of our island society regarding people with disabilities.

We may be somewhat unusual
We may not be your type
But be assured, we are human,
So don't deny us our rights.

We're a little slow at learning
Yet, sensitive to care
We are capable of feeling,
Bouts of sadness, love or cheer.

CHS:
So we are all of God's creatures
See what we've got deep inside.
Just don't see our imperfections
But the courage in our stride.

We are not to be discarded
From our society
But when our goals are set before us,
We challenge them daringly.

We send this plea to our nation
Provide with a chance
To share our warmth and affection,
Help us take our rightful stance

On the other hand, I now work in a geriatric home at a job that allows me to minister to residents by performing it with prayer and love to seniors. There is no singing and no entertaining involved. I just comfort ailing elderly people in their time of need. I provide the skilled care in my area of expertise, with the love of God. Sometimes a gentle empathetic word, patience to listen to a scared, frail soul, a gentle touch or a soothing word can minister to a scared or angry person with far-reaching effects. There are many hurting people in this world, who benefit from the ministry of helps so never underestimate this ministry. You never know where life may take you but wherever you land, Jesus will always make you ***relevant***.

CHAPTER FOUR

THE BEST OF TIMES

The best investment dad made in life was *'making memories'* with us. My dad taught us how to get away from our rigid demands and lifestyle and just have fun. He knew the pressures placed on us from church, school and work because He felt them too. He was great at bending the rules without breaking them and he taught us how to play. He taught us not to take life too seriously and prevented some major family meltdowns. In a home of over-crowding, he must have known when we were getting to the point of meltdown. He would often take us to the beach for hours and days at a time. Here is the twist, he would take off of work, stop off at home and get mom (who would have cooked a hot delicious one-pot meal in her iron pot), and then swing around each child's school and take us all out of school. He played by the rules but he did not let the law get in the way of our freedom and love for life. He deflated life's pressures by teaching us how to stop and smell the salt air, so to speak. My head mistress and teachers would be infuriated in their uptight way but he was the parent and had the right to take us out of school. We were not failing at our studies and we had the right to live life to the fullest. It used to be a great break for my parents as well. I think they needed the privacy and solitude just as much as we did. Aah family time! With such a large family and people in and out of our home, overcrowding was just part of our daily lives. Our beds were over crowded with either, siblings or strangers, multiple family members trying to get into two bathrooms and two shower stalls, too many of us at one kitchen table, too many loud noises and distractions to get any quality studying done for school and too many opinionated kids who would yell loudly, just to be noticed and be heard. There was even overcrowding in the car but that was fun overcrowding when we piled on top of each other to get to the beach. The windows of the car would be down and the wind would be rushing through blowing our hair and hitting our little faces. Alone time with my parents and siblings, YES I loved it! You could not believe the jokes, the insults between siblings, and the wonderful fights for the passenger seats next to the window, as there was no air conditioning in the car. Now that was *normal!* Surprise people we are not having prayer meetings and bible study at home each day!

For short precious moments, we would know the meaning of normalcy, family and total abandon. There would be no prying eyes, no judgmental consequences and no hang-ups. We could be kids, as rowdy and obnoxious, as our parents would allow. There were even occasional profane words among the siblings, when the going got rough. We would hope the other sibling would not squeal to dad and mom as we experimented with "naughty words". Of course, the other siblings were experimenting too and it sure was an ace for future blackmail among us. I do not condone cursing and this language repulses me, but the reality is we experimented among ourselves. I do not know why but we did, that was just the reality. I guess because it was something we were not supposed to do so we did it. Maybe the bad words fit the bill for our explosive personalities. Maybe, just maybe, we felt safest with each other and could trust each other. We had to know for sure that we would safeguard each other's hearts with our 'good' and 'bad' stuff, no judgments attached. I really cannot give any further reasons as I am not a psychologist. It was part of our childhood dynamic and sibling development. I even remember when my cousin Shelly met her husband. She needed my confidence and trust. I knew her parents would disapprove of this relationship but this was the sibling code of honor. My cousin needed my trust when there was no one else to trust, whether it was misplaced, misguided or wrong. To this day, she trusts me. To this day whether any of my siblings or cousins fight or embrace, we have the bond of trust among ourselves.

Anyway, back to our family moments. I remember during our car trips my dad bursting into song. Picture a tone-deaf preacher singing. We would tease him but he did not care. He would happily sing out of tune all the way to our destination. Mom would teach us her childhood songs and we would sing in rounds. Lord knows there were a lot of us piled in that old car, which would result in songs with three sets of rounds sung at the same time. As you can imagine each group of kids tried to outdo the other and it would be wonderfully loud. Mom would tell us such outrageous family jokes and she would have to get her 'puffer' because she would laugh until she wheezed. We only had each other for entertainment, as there were no ipods, cell phones, DS games, Nintendo portable electronics or anything of the sort. Back then, we really had to interact with each other. The trips were so long we would often become peckish and Dad gave us an appreciation for eating roasted corn at the roadside; enjoy a drink from a cold coconut cut by a man with a huge machete. On the way back from the beach he would take us to an upscale hotel and indulge us in fine dining while in our beach clothes. Let me share more details of freedom with you. The drives were very long as beaches are at least one and a half hours away and longer, with narrow winding roads. Most times, we would fall asleep leaning on each other after the exhilaration of escaping school, laughing with mom and singing many songs. Suddenly, the feel and smell of the air would change and we would pop up to the grandeur. The air would have a wonderful fresh, crisp salty fragrance you only smell at an island beach. It would arouse us all from sleep and bring renewed life. We would immediately have a shift in perspective as our minds and bodies would immediately relax. The change in scenery would totally consume us. There is nothing like awakening to miles of coconut tree-lined roads broken by strips of blue ocean and white-crested waves from the breaking surf on the shoreline. Before long, we would burst out in shouts of laughter upon hearing the increasingly loud pounding of surf and the distant squeals of the seagulls. We would be at our destination, Freedom. Before dad could turn off the engine, we would all rush out of the car at the same time, tumbling over each other, with sweet abandon. The spray of the surf would instantly spritz our little faces, as though welcoming the family; and we would run up to the water's edge feeling the tickle of the bubbly salty water. Fresh air, limitless space and the majestic pounding surf of the ocean would free us in a miraculous way. The smell of the salty air at the ocean would instantly bring calm to my heart and I would immediately join nature in magnifying God. I would lift my hands in the air, twirl and declare the glories of God. To this day, I get to the beach and I instantly go into worship. Nature in its state of grandeur magnifies the majesty and greatness of God. There were no prying eyes to judge us, no one censuring our behaviors, no one placing limitations on us. Dad would immediately, in his 'falling down' shorts and Bermuda hat, set up his most beloved rope hammock and fall into it with ease to rest. He and mom would rest under the coconut trees, fall asleep and allow us to play for hours. Swimming became the ultimate experience when our dad got into the water. Screams of delight and joy would fly through the air. He was the world's greatest swimmer. He would glide through the waves like a sleek shark, conquering them with little effort. He would swim way past the breakers until we could not see him. All of a sudden without seeing dad return, we would feel something grab hold of our feet and would scream out of surprise and fright. Somehow, 'shark dad' was able to swim right back to us in the shallow water, hide and then play tricks on us. He was so strong! He could pick up two kids at a time and throw us high into the air and into the welcoming, tumbling surf. We felt pure joy and delight with our dad. He was fully ours for this moment and we did not have to share him. He would enjoy us with total abandonment. No one could win a water fight with him even though he would take on all four and eventually six kids, over the years. He would start the fight off with a slow little tap of the water to our faces and smile. We would think we could let him have it and would shove ton loads of water at him with all our strength and might. He would let us think we were weakening him, but then his eyes would widen and his face would appear mockingly fierce. He would begin to splash us vigorously and the crescendo would increase as he would eventually use both hands and we would be unable to tolerate that much water in our faces and ultimately give up. We would collapse onto the welcoming bubbly surf, out of exhaustion. Even as adults, no one ever beat dad at water fighting. To this day, these are moments we still recall and savor among ourselves. They were even sweeter because they happened on days when we should have all been in school or at work.

Every evening when the family sat around the table dad would pray over the meal. It became a standing joke because we would inform him that we were very hungry and this was not a church service. Dad would purposely initiate with a long prayer of thanksgiving. We would become fidgety, start teasing each other at the table, open our eyes and fool around while dad was earnestly praying. He would eventually peek at us with one eye open, sensing our outlandish behaviors and continue praying smilingly, until we egged him on to stop. It would end with howls of laughter at the table. I know we were unrighteous and irreverent but we all had fun. Dad never took himself too seriously and he was never self-righteous.

The most self-affirming moment in life came when my dad totally validated my value for the family circle. It was the last time he spoke to us around our family Christmas tree. Dad loved the concept of Christmas and all its traditions and splendor, a kid at heart. I waited to hear him say the things he said that night, all my life. He told us he learned the most important lesson of a lifetime. He said, 'FAMILY IS

THE MOST IMPORTANT THING IN THIS WORLD.' He went on to share that, '. . . at the end of the day, family members are the only ones who are there for each other . . . If I had the chance to live my life over again, I would spend more time with you guys.' My heart flipped when I heard him say this. Whoa, was my hearing off! He affirmed that our family bond was more valuable than anything he achieved in this world. I waited all my life to hear those words from dad even though I knew how important ministry was to him. There I was sitting on the living room floor, holding on to my precious eighteen-month old baby and thinking she is the most important human being on the planet to me. I needed dad to feel that way about me, about all of us.

Anyway, I have to explain this one in order for you to get how mind-blowing this moment was for me. You see, this was a man, who never let a moment bypass him. He wasted no time and achieved something every waking moment of his life. He did not have many educational opportunities when he was a child so he valued education and work. He lived to serve to his town, his country and most importantly, Jesus and his parishioners, never counting the personal, emotional or physical cost. He loved us and cared for us but we definitely had a designated place in his life. Well he went on to say that, 'a man's greatest treasure and investment is his family.' This came from a man who was a pioneer in the formation of many congregations, a theologian and a community leader. It came from a dad who adored his family and gave each child the honor of being 'daddy's favorite' now six of us no less. He did not even realize that he did all that he could have done for us. He never once neglected us, yet towards the end of his life, he felt as though somehow he did. He was never forceful but somehow we knew our place. It was the unwritten rule that church people came first. At this moment however, he needed to let us know that our place was supposed to be first with him. He let us know that he should have been a dad first and we were entitled to his full attention. It sounded like a final life statement to the family and it was, even though we did not know it at the time. He spoke to the entire extended family of aunts, cousins, children, grandchildren next-door neighbors, spouses and boyfriends, as well as close friends. He insisted that we should all know Christ in an intimate way and we should love each other without reservation. He insisted in a tone of finality, that we should invest in our eternal destiny and reach for Heaven so that the family circle will never be broken.

Parents of PKs:

Today I guard my family with my life. In my humble opinion, if a minister saves everyone in the world from damnation, build huge churches, facilitate the reconciliation of a million marriages, forgive the unforgivable, feed the poor, give world renown sermons but loses one of his or her precious children to Hell, it would not be worth the journey! I ask you ministers, how would you feel if you saved the world from eternal torment and lose your children forever? Wow, talk about successful ministry there brothers and sisters! Whether it takes you a lifetime, your children's salvation, are the most important conversions of your ministry. How could any preacher stand before Christ and account for his or her children being lost to eternal damnation, and do no give me the Peter giving it all up for Christ! Preachers you ARE ACCOUNTABLE! You have a mandate to, *[train up you children in the ways of the Lord so that when they are at the age of maturity they will not depart from Him] Prov. 22:6.*

This verse does not mean taking your kids to church all the time, forcing them into 'ministry' and beating them over the head with a Bible, so to speak. No, that is not the way. Being a preacher's kid and a mom, I can only share with you what I think. At this point, I am not quite diligent in getting my daughter to Sunday school every single Sunday, working on that. It is important however to teach you child the ways of the Lord in daily life. For instance, a prayer of thanksgiving before each meal is awesome in my house. I have exposed my daughter to needy children of the world. It has moved my daughter to empathetic tears. Some in North America think that, that exposure was too severe. Well guess what, she was three at the time and when it was her turn to pray at dinner, it was better and more heartfelt than any preacher's prayer. My three-year old daughter did not need a script but prayed with her own words. She prayed that, Jesus would give the needy children houses, mommies and daddies, and all the good toys and stuff that she had. How awesome is that! She told me, 'mom call American Idol, and give them money so the children can get help'. She was moved and empathetic to the needs of those who were hurting. She cried when she saw the hurting children. She listened to the still small voice of the Holy Spirit. Today she ministers to the poor by gathering her clothes and shoes for the kids in need. When purchasing something for herself she will purchase new things for needy children. There you go preachers a simple childlike awareness becomes a ministry of helps, with no prompting from me her mom. There are no prayer scripts just a sensitive prayer to Jesus. When things go wrong, or someone in our family is ill, she knows we must go to our loving Father in prayer. My child has learned thankfulness and appreciation for her daily bread. She frequently tells my husband and me, 'I appreciate you and everything you do for me'. She is now nine years old and has learned the power and the blessing of honoring her parents at a tender age. Guess what, we have not beaten her to death with guilt and shame but have extended loving care and nurturing, as the Father cares for us. I am sure teenage years will be challenging but there is prayer. *'. . . the effectual fervent prayer of the righteous man availeth much." Jam. 5:16.*

Pray for your children every day, that means pray for them *'without ceasing' I Thess. 5:17*, just as the Bible states. Each day should be another step in their personal walk towards the Father. This in turn will make them sensitive to the still small voice of the Holy Spirit. Yes ministers, you do have a heavenly script, and that is to pray for your children and love them unconditionally.

Just guide them along the way when they make their decisions regarding education, career and life partners. Show them unconditional love when it matters and provide guidance when they need to stop and think, before making a life-decision. Let God's Light shine through your parenting when your children become distracted and off course by the world and its influences. Pray the Word into their lives. Jesus was great while He was with us on earth but self-righteous was never one of his traits. Let your children know you are Christians by your love for them. Light shines brightest and love is strongest, during dark and unforgiving moments. Maybe just maybe, if you are training your children to see Christ in simple everyday things, they may choose to cling to Truth and Light. I rest my case.

PKs:

Hey kids, *[we are a chosen generation (not just called) and a royal priesthood 1Pet.2:9.]* which means, we have all been enlisted with Jesus for *intimacy and war*. Just find your position in God it is that simple. You do not come with a full-proof manual so give your parents a break. They are trying to hide you and protect you from the Evil One. They might be a little clumsy in their approach but their ultimate motivation is their love for you, which they believe, God's Love makes perfect. They ultimately want you to be happy and avoid pitfalls in life that can steal years of your life and even destroy you eternally. There is no more time to waste. Capture the perishing, and pull them back from eternal death and suffering. Quickly get it together without compromise. You are strong and well trained. This is your time and your generation. Why let it pass without taking it by storm. You too will be accountable for this time and your life choices. It works both ways. The King is coming soon, whose side are you on? Do not spend time wallowing in past pigpen experiences. Let God do His perfect work of salvation and grace within you. Know that you are God's inheritance and work towards your destiny with His guidance through the Word. Let his Love free you from your fears, hurts and insecurities. Let your future vision cause you to press forward and upward, instead of allowing past mistakes to pull down your dreams and destiny in Christ. There is healing in the wings of Jesus, if you choose to let Him transform you moment by moment.

CHAPTER FIVE

A LITTLE CHURCH POLITICS
GOES A LONG WAY

I am a survivor of brutal organizational wars within a once reputable church organization that tore down great Fathers of Faith and Men of Honor. Organizational boardroom politics negatively affected my family, because of in-house ministerial fights among once 'trusted' ministers. I am the child of a preacher man, who has had to survive ruthless lies and tyranny, among young preachers driven by greed for power, money as well as political and social agendas. I witnessed my gentle loving father defend his honor as well as the honor of other great men of God. To protect his ministry, his family, other men of God as well as the sheep he had to become creative and engage in undercover espionage. This innocent gentle man was so intimidated that he investigated and purchased a hidden pen recorder, to take with him to board meetings because young greedy ministers conjured up lies against him and the presiding organizational headship. Their aim was to overthrow the leaders who were sitting on the National Board of Directors of this formerly great church organization. Did they not remember the verses from *1 Tim. 5:1, 17-18,* on honor and ordination? *"Rebuke not an elder, but entreat him as a father . . . Let the elders that rule well be counted worthy of double honor, especially they who labor in the word and doctrine . . . . The laborer is worthy of his reward . . . Against an elder receive not an accusation . . ."*

The directors of this organization were in their rightful seats after years of labor, sacrifice, training and experience on the battlefields. Could you believe they accused these Founding Fathers of Faith of homosexuality, adultery, political and financial corruption? These young ministers did not choose to learn from the great ministers who forged ministries under rum shops, (bars), stilted wooden homes and open-air street meetings. These young ministers with their ungodly agendas displaced the Founding Fathers and placed themselves in positions of authority and headship. There was no respect, no humility, no accountability, no seat of learning, no regard for discipline and service because they did not know their place in the Body of Christ. They disregarded the protocol the apostle Paul outlined for leadership and apostleship in *1 Tim. 3:2-6 "A bishop then must be blameless, the husband of one wife, vigilant, sober of good behaviors, given to hospitality, apt to teach; not given to wine, no striker, not greedy of filthy lucre; but patient not a brawler, not covetous; One that ruleth well his own house, having his children subjection with all gravity; (For if a man know not how to rule his own house, how shall he take care of the church of God?) Not a novice, lest being lifted up with pride he fall into condemnation of the devil."* They craved to ascend to power and leadership roles without God's anointing, appointment or sanction. These young ministers threw away sound foundational truths from the Word of God. They put aside scriptures from *Heb. 5:1 and 4,* which states, *"For every high priest taken from among men is ordained for men in things pertaining to God, that he may offer both gifts and sacrifices for sins." "And no man taketh this honor unto himself, but he that is called of God, as was Aaron."* They all forgot Aaron's ordination *Ex. 30:30-33* that states," *. . . And thou shalt anoint Aaron and his sons, and consecrate them, that they may minister unto me in the priest's office. And thou shalt speak unto the children of Israel, saying, This shall be an holy anointing oil unto me throughout your generations. Upon man's flesh shall it not be poured, neither shall ye make any other like it, after the composition of it: it is holy, and it shall be holy unto you. Whosoever compoundeth any like it, or whosoever putteth any of it upon a stranger, shall even be cut off from his people."*

It was a sad and disappointing day, when each church within this part of the Bride was taken over by greedy men who had no order or regard for authority, nor did they care about the effects on the children of God. The young ministers were not content to *[do the work of an evangelist first, and make full proof of their ministry. 1 Tim 4:5].* These men were the sort that crept into the houses of God as robbers and thieves. It was anarchy between our wise, experienced ministers and young rebellious, covetous preachers, who felt entitled to 'take over the reins.' Eventually discord and rebellion, filtered down from the national boardroom to the churches. It resulted in the ripping apart of every single congregation within the organization. The now corrupt leadership was using the sheep as pawns for the destruction of each pastor. They instructed these dissidents to be loud and vulgar. I watched in horrific disbelief, as people who my parents counseled, loved and trained for Jesus for years, incited others to rebellion in the House of the Lord. Across every congregation, the few rebellious ones were trained well, to disrupt services with verbal outbursts and attacks. Congregants were open to the seduction of these rebels. We witnessed

The Word come to life. *11 Tim. 4: 3, 4 "For the time will come when they will not endure sound doctrine; but after their own lusts shall they heap to themselves teachers, having itching ears; And they shall turn away their ears from the truth, and shall be turned to fables."* In my mind, I wondered what kind of headship would allow such sacrilege in our sacred houses of worship. Congregants wailed and bawled as lies from accusers were crawling out of the mouths of these rebels. The Bride shook as the winds of turmoil blew and systematically raged on. Brothers and sisters in the Lord became divided and confused. There was split loyalty within church membership with rifts and strife dividing families. These were the same families with whom my parents would spend hours, at the cost of their own family time. The accusers were people dad and mom continually held up in prayer, counseled and spent hours ensuring their illiterate family members were properly educated. This scene took place throughout the nation in each of our congregations, with varying degrees of volatility. These actions became the personification of *11 Tim.3:3,4 identifying, [false accusers, covetous, boasters, trucebreakers, blasphemers, traitors, highmindedness and despisers of good . . . Having a form of godliness . . ., ever learning and never able to come to the knowledge of the truth.]* At the First Church, the headquarters of the organization, the scandal rocked the neighborhood as rebels brought in prior founding missionaries to attack the presiding pastor. They yelled and brawled on the microphone and the entire neighborhood came out of their houses in shock and awe. They heard every miserable, vile word from the same place they heard weekly sermons, worship and the gospel of grace and love. This was not cleaning house and this was not order and decorum. The spirit of witchcraft prevailed for a short season and invaded every congregation, as *[rebellion is as the sin of witchcraft I Sam. 15:23.]*

Dad always preserved our souls and spirits by conducting counsel in the privacy of the church office or in the needy family's home. He never exposed us to the words of vicious people, as he was a wise diplomatic pastor. He knew our tender little hearts could not fully comprehend the sordid and complicated matters of adulthood and sin. Unfortunately, dad was unable to protect us fully from the evil that pervaded our congregations and homes, during this rebellious season.

The obscene behaviors did not stop within the church doors. I could clearly remember a Saturday morning when we were all at home. I was washing the family's laundry on the cement sink with its built-in scrub board. We did not yet have a washing machine and mom's health was too fragile to scrub the family's clothing and linens; as the asthma she often incurred would be debilitating. This was a typical Saturday at home when we were not off at a beach somewhere on the island. The kids were noisily playing with each other and enjoying the hot day in the backyard, with birds chirping as they picked on ripe fruit. Dogs were barking throughout the neighborhood and mom and dad were inside enjoying their lazy Saturday morning breakfast, chuckling at something or other. Before long, a white car pulled up outside of our joyful home, which was a typical scenario. Someone was always interrupting our family time outside of church hours. Thinking nothing of it, I casually walked down to the front gate in my sopping wet dress and asked how I could help this person. It turned out to be one of the church rebels who made a scene in church the Sunday prior. He was eerily quiet and I mistook this behavior to mean he was penitent for the disruption in church. My heart was hopeful at this moment. Deep within me though, I must have been on guard and unaware of it but I did not invite him in, nor did I unlock the black wrought iron gate. I told him to wait where he was and I will get my dad. From the moment my dad approached the gate, this man became wild, screaming obscenities and verbal accusations that were unbelievable. We all stood back on our little cemented porch and stared. The joyful noise of children at play became still, my mom's laughter turned into silent anger and disbelief. All of a sudden, the only things one could hear were the occasional car driving by, a dog barking in the distance and birds chirping. Above all this background noise, the man's loud voice bellowed in the foreground of our ears and souls. He was so loud and boisterous; our neighbor came out to witness this deplorable scene and inquired of my dad if he should call the police. My dad refused the offer and told my neighbor he would handle this situation and he did. He was strong, fearless and protective of us all. My short five foot, two inch dad changed his boyish, carefree stride. He approached this evil with his shoulders thrown back, his understated stocky well-built chest, (from years of swimming in the ocean) pushed out and his back erect. His chest was big enough to accommodate hugs simultaneously from his four and ultimately six

49

children. His short little legs became the legs of a soldier marching into battle, with each forceful stride decreasing the distance between he and evil. His face was serious and resilient and he did not break stride or eye contact with this pathetic man. 'How dare this man come on our precious sanctified property to desecrate our home and our family?' This was a place of joy and learning and extensive creativity. This was a precious home with the extended family, my grandparents the patriarchs ensuring our salvation throughout each generation with much prayer, love and discipline. My dad had already been a minister for years and faced many physical, emotional and spiritual giants and demons. This warlock, who warmed the church benches for a long time, was no match for my dad, a true man of God. It reminds me today of the scripture in *11 Tim. 2:20 "But in a great house there are not only vessels of gold and of silver, but also of wood and of earth; and some to honour, and some to dishonour."* With the supreme authority of Holy Spirit dad easily subdued this man. With the authority of an appointed leader, my dad dismissed him as he would a demon! Like a stern father, my dad with a strong unwavering voice told him to respect our home and speak in quieter tones, as he was standing next to him. This made Mr. Gan angrier. He began using profanity at my father, his nostrils flaring, arms and hands flailing around. Of course, kids always hear the curse words and they stunned us! I wondered how this so-called Christian man's anger could propel him to use foul language at this respected man of God. We were dumbfounded and shocked! Until this time, no one had ever spoken to my dad in such a foul manner and loud tone. We never heard such horrid language before. Dad was not shocked for a minute, as he was the manager of our meat and fish abattoir, and worked among butchers and fishermen, people who killed animals for a living. These men looked like big brutes to be quite honest. He managed the street sweepers of our town and the sellers within The town's produce market. He would often take us with him to his places of work to meet the people and see where our foods came from. Yet, in all the years that he supervised the town markets, day laborers, the butchers and the fishermen, they all spoke to him tenderly and with great respect. Whenever someone came to the house, no matter how poor, dirty or uneducated he or she would approach my dad with respectful words and a humble stance. They were bigger, stronger and meaner than this man was, and they could have sliced dad into pieces if they chose but these people honored my dad. In fact, they were thankful to him for his gentle demeanor and all the energy he spent getting the town to hire them. They appreciated his work ethic, his Christian love and his continual fight for them in the Town Hall.

The little man at the gate only had a big mouth. He was so loud most of his words were distorted but we got wind of some key words like 'hate', 'liar', 'thief', 'adulterer' which were punctuated with frequent words of profanity. Dad was unaware that the vipers that came out of Gan's mouth slithered into our home and began attacking my spirit. My dad could not stop the slithering vipers as they were attacking our minds and spirits, as we were, witnesses to that moment and vile interchange. We were actually in the right place at the wrong time. Some of my younger siblings underwent some type of spiritual transformation as well, with varying degrees. I remember the ugly gold tooth inserted in his mouth, as it caught the reflection of the sun causing it to gleam mockingly at us each time he opened his mouth. Nothing golden and uplifting came out of his mouth. It was pure filth and unfounded vile accusations of robbery and adultery! He was so overtaken by hate that the admonition in *1 Tim. 2:5, "But shun profane and vain babblings: for they will increase unto more ungodliness"* could not echo in his heart nor convict his spirit. When dad could not get the man to quiet down, he lifted his arm towards the direction from which the man came. With the anointing of the prophets of old, he commanded the man to leave the property instantly. There was power in that stance and authority echoing from his strong unwavering voice of declaration. This was a supernatural war. You may be wondering how I knew this was supernatural warfare at such a young age. It is simple, the reaction of the man was the same as when demons react to prayer and anointed declarations to leave someone's possessed soul, a phenomenon that was a norm in my parents' ministry. The man screamed angrily, recoiled as though dad hit him physically and he fled the property, never returning to church after that day. He never had a chance to bait my dad into a physical fight because God (I did not perceive it then), did not allow me to unlock that gate. That was my first realization that this warfare was beyond the natural. Our land and home, which were dedicated to God and purchased with prayer, sacrificial love, and hard toil, underwent a day of desecration. The man brought a spirit of defilement to innocent spirits, even though dad removed him from our property. I felt that moment deep within my gut, my heart and my mind. It is a marked moment in the realm of time. Eternity documented this moment, as it was a turning point of stolen childhood innocence, as I was old enough to process this evil from a young teenage perspective. This evil also hurt some of my siblings even though some were too young to express such a complicated inner change. The corporate far-reaching effects on the family, was my second realization that spiritual warfare occurred. Unfortunately, we did witness the viciousness, the hateful lies and the rebellious behaviors.

I was too young to perceive this situation as I do today but I can pinpoint this moment as another significant moment in my spiritual downward spiral. The betrayal and hatred were so great on our tender lives that some of us, including me, fell away from loving and serving Christ. I remained an obedient and submissive child to the will of my parents and extended family, most of them ministers, until I could leave home. I did not want ministry nor did I want to see anyone experience salvation, healing or deliverance from demons. Unfortunately, I can honestly admit I stopped caring. Recently while writing this book and identifying my fall from grace this moment has become my third realization that Evil invaded our lives and it did not only come for my parents but for their children. I wanted people to leave me alone. Sad to admit, I hated people and I would constantly say that to my dad with gentler words, of course. I would tell him, 'People fail you every time.' I would tell him that the investment in people was not worth a hoot. I tried to stay away from people. I did not want to talk to them, I did not want friendships and I certainly did not want them forced on me. I only trusted myself. I knew I alone, could take care of my heart and ensure people would never have the power to hurt me. This was a difficult stance to take when my parents pressed into humanity even further with greater love and anointing. I served with resentment and bitterness under my parents' ministry and if I am to be honest, I served with hatred in my heart for people, for which I am thoroughly repentant. I unfortunately allowed the evils of hatred and pride to seethe throughout my being and into adulthood. I allowed the polar opposite spirit of God's Love to take over and grip me like a vice. I gave up my heart and control to the evil spirit of Hatred, everything the Spirit of Christ is not. I would smile and speak patronizingly to people because I had to serve; meanwhile thinking, 'who do these people think they are to demand my parents love and attention, our service and sacrifice.' I became everything Jesus never wanted anyone to be, 'hateful' the very thing for which He conquered Hell and Death. It was destructive to me as my intimacy with the Father experienced a great divide. In retrospect, I exposed myself to Evil without the protection of the armor of God. Hatred and bitterness have cost me years of intimacy with Jesus and the relationship eventually grew lukewarm. I felt my attitude about people was increasingly justified, each time some poor soul stumbled, during his or her walk of sanctification to the Father. Mr. Gan had served Evil well as Evil took ahold of me. Other than my siblings, cousins and extended family members, I wanted no one. The casualties of this once vicious war were preachers, preachers' kids and preachers' families. We the preachers' kids became the ultimate price of this organizational war. We became the dying souls, as many of us strayed away from God and ministry and no one tried to rescue us. There was no one to bandage the wounds and minister to our broken bleeding bodies, our confused, crippled minds and our defeated spirits. There were no 'Good Samaritans'. Everyone else was either, crippled by the blows or moved on to other denominational congregations, without a backward glance. The church left us to heal ourselves as best we could and our lives became succulent juice for holy gossipers, who pointed their fingers with self-righteous 'they should know better' comments. They jeered at our confused state as we stumbled around to find ourselves and restore our wholeness in the Lord. How sad is this, my church friends, family of God. Learn from the battlefields and casualties of the past.

The new so-called 'men of God', who were now in leadership, disgusted me. Instead of forgiveness, I harbored malice in my heart towards them. During my young teenage years, I unknowingly measured their behaviors by the standard of God's Word but I did not apply God's Spirit of Truth, forgiveness and love to these leaders and people. His Spirit was not in the mutiny I thought and things were out of order and Godly alignment. I remember my tender faith, instantly becoming battered and broken, which put me into an immediate identity crisis. Up until this point, my 'faith' was my spiritual DNA, defining my person, my innermost being, my sense of self. Instantly I lost my identity and wholeness. I also remember asking dad, how was it he believed in this gospel when those we trust did not display the love of Christ and the fruits of the Spirit. I felt that this faith was not authentic and Christianity was a hoax. I thought to myself, if this 'faith' were real, this travesty would not have happened. I even remember telling dad that maybe I would explore the old Hindu religious beliefs, as they seemed peaceful. I told him that I could not believe that these trusted men whom we loved, could become vicious loud-mouthed vipers. I saw no love of Jesus here. Dad was patient with me through this devastating confusion. He never tried to coerce my faith in God but instead, displayed love, grace, purity, steadfastness and strength. He tolerated my quips about fake preachers and my statement that I was my own person with no need for God. I lost respect for most ministers. I lost Hope and became a disoriented soul. I questioned Jesus' love and faithfulness wondering why He allowed this terrible thing to happen. All the while, my dad showed he was a true Christian by love, the love of God, which permanently sealed his heart. That was his greatest testimony to his children. He rose above the storm. My dad, mom and many of the founding ministers felt humiliated by these evil actions but they displayed steadfastness and strength in God. They remained, *[steadfast and unmovable and they abounded in the work of the Lord and in Him their labor was not in vain] 1 Cor. 15:58.* These true men and women of God went on to achieve victory in continued service to Jesus. Strong ministries were born out of this monumental organizational divide. This was a testament of Faith in God against the wiles of the enemy! They all kept 'standing' amidst the storm that raged around them on every side and for many years.

Since that time, few of us lucky ones have survived these so called 'men of God' who tried to destroy our parents' their dignity, reputation and ministries; which were born out of years of personal toil and family sacrifice. I have seen many of my counterparts and their families broken, disillusioned, crushed and humiliated before their congregations, throughout the nation. Unfortunately, some of the families and children have taken the long way Home. Some have returned to the fold but others still live with unhealed battle scars. We need to rescue these lost children, now adults, from this past battleground of deadly war and *never forget.* We must never indulge in forgetfulness of our maimed and dying brothers and sisters, who are still perishing out there on a past battlefield. We must not forget, so that we will relentlessly pursue each of these souls, until they return to Jesus, to Love.

Preachers and Congregants:

In the arena of religious politics, your tongues can be as whips on the backs of preachers' kids. Your words can cause deadly consequences, against them. Remember, *[life and death are in the tongue and they that love it shall eat the fruit thereof—Prov. 18:21.]* Fellow Christians, when you are in disagreement with the leadership, the preachers' kids are not whipping posts and pawns for boardroom blackmail. Churches are not commodities with which to barter. The church is a living person, the Bride. She belongs to no man but her Heavenly Bridegroom. The structures are our homes to congregate corporately and celebrate the Almighty. Administrators, leaders, preachers, deacons and board members, the Bride is not yours! Do not think you can ravish her and know your place! You are her stewards, you are only the 'best man' and your duties are to serve the Bridegroom; ensuring that the Bride is preserved until she can present herself in white garments to her Groom. She is not to be raped, plundered or violated. You are accountable to the Father for your stewardship, so leaders I urge you to know your place in Christ. The Father will judge you harshly if she is not perfect or she becomes defiled while under your stewardship. We are not harlots for sale but the virtuous Bride of Christ. *"Let no corrupt speech, proceed out of your mouth, but such as is good for edifying as the need may be, that it may give grace to them that hear. And grieve not the Holy Spirit of God, in whom ye were sealed unto the day of redemption. Let all bitterness, and wrath, and anger, and clamor, and railing, be put away from you, and all malice: and be ye kind one to another, tenderhearted, forgiving each other, even as God also in Christ forgave you." Eph.4: 29-32.* Your words and actions against these kids are violent and powerful acts. I look around and my peers are going through similar situations as I did but with greater intensity than I ever experienced, as humanity is quickly spinning out of control. Christians are becoming 'churchgoers' and reactions to others are less dictated by Holy Spirit, as the church becomes desensitized. It is *not okay* for us to accept that the preachers' kids are heading out of church into a lost, damned eternity.

'Eternity' people, goes on and on with no end. If the worst of sinners deserve salvation from eternal damnation, these young souls also have the right to full evangelism. They do not deserve to inherit eternal torment because of idle words and actions that have hurt them. When young preachers' kids experience unexpected malice from Christians who should exemplify God's love, the impact can be destructive. Careless words and actions can have detrimental consequences to these little ones, whose spiritual foundation is not yet fully established or mature. These tender reeds can bend and break if they are unprotected, when battered by the demonic storms that can rage within churches. These are the 'formative years' for young preachers' kids, to coin one of my grandmother's Maisims. Keep in mind reader, *"And whoso shall cause one of these little ones that believe on me to stumble, it is profitable for him that a great millstone should be hanged about his neck, and he should be sunk in the depth of the sea" Matt.18:6.* Tread softly around these souls for you just might be *[touching God's anointed, and doing His prophets harm] Chron. 16:22,* which can be a place 'where angels fear to tread' (to use the book title by E. M. Forster, 1905).

PK's:

This is dedicated to all the children who inherit the *[the prize of the high calling (Phil. 3:14)].* Hey, my counterparts out there, whether you believe it or not, this *"high calling"* is a *"prize"*, ours to inherit and claim. No one should ever steal our right as a joint heir of Christ. *". . . be strong in the Lord, and in the power of his might." Eph 6:10.* Let us defend our birthright with joy, praise and violence. By that I mean, *[Put on the whole armor of God that you may be able to stand against the wiles of the devil . . . . the Helmet of Salvation, the Breastplate of Righteousness and the Shield of Faith to quench the fiery darts of the evil one. Let your loins be girded up with Truth, your feet be shod with the preparation of the Gospel of Peace and carry The Sword of the Spirit, which is the Word of God]. Eph. 6:11-17;* yep, that is what I mean by defending the Kingdom with violence. We must defend our heritage and take back our birthright. Words of malice, contradictions and accusations, are some of the effective *'principalities, powers and wickedness' (Eph. 6:12),* used against us. We need to guard ourselves, as these words can cut so deeply we can fall and never get up. The armor of God is critical covering, if we are going to stand strong during raging battles. Defend God's love within you, otherwise it will be replaced by demonic spirits of hate and bitterness; causing a breech, with the Lover of your soul. Remember, ***". . . NOW are ye light in the Lord: walk as children of light." Eph. 5:8.*** If we use the armor of Jesus' love and wisdom, evil weapons lose their effectiveness to steal, kill and destroy our lives.

CHAPTER SIX

LIFE'S MISTAKES-OH YES WE HAVE THEM TOO

To add to our confusion while growing up, I felt issues of virginity and sexual morality prematurely came into the mix. The church leadership distorted and mishandled these issues. I think some of the parishioners were more obsessed with sex and morality, than the teenagers were. This added another layer to the already mounting pressure by the church population to conform to their standards, for fear we would not fit into their neatly boxed-in world. To be honest until they brought it up, we had not given it much thought, if any at all. I think some of the girls in church, eventually became pregnant early in life because there was an obsessive emphasis on 'sex' and 'fornication.' That was just too much premature information and pressure! God forbid if you even thought about going out for a simple date during your teenage years. There were no resources for the young Christian on responsible Christian courtship, no protocol for Christian dating, and no practical counsel on coming-of-age issues. I think the fear and dictatorial approach of the leaders, led the teenagers to explore. By that I mean, the overemphasis of the evils of sex, mystified the issue and stimulated teenage curiosity, instead of putting it into its rightful coming-of-age perspective. The leadership did not offer productive alternatives on which we could focus and our now aroused curiosity regarding sex and its evils, exploded. The warnings simply fanned the kids' curiosity and inflamed teenage hormones. There was no productive guidance for the kids. This futile approach resulted in unwanted premature marriages and pregnancies, many of which have now ended in divorces today. Yup you heard me, **DIVORCES**.

Let me take you back to 1982 when I was eighteen years old. While stupidly trying to assert some kind of control and independence, I decided to announce my intentions to wed, hah, what a joke on me, and a costly one at that! I thought I would have the love and respect of a good, strong 'Christian' man, and make decisions independent of my parents and the church. I thought I would *find* myself, and boy did I find myself! I found myself in an absolute mess! Firstly, we were not even allowed to date, period! Against my parents' wishes and without their blessing I went ahead and got married too young. I am sure if I had the opportunity to date and discover what the man was really like, I would not have pursued the relationship at all. In my own stupid head, the only way to explore a relationship with the opposite sex, without discrediting my father's reputation and mine, was within the institution of marriage. Boy was I totally misguided! Well marriage dealt me quite a blow with some huge complex problems I could not foresee (being so very young and idiotic). I faced huge relationship and emotional crises but initially rose to the challenge with all the vigor of youth. Marriage should be two people living life as one unit. Well as years went by I was forced to admit I was alone and lonely in this marriage. I was the only one actively participating in building this new life. In hindsight, I have since discovered that I can live alone but not be lonely. Eventually this unhealthy and unblessed marriage crumbled into pieces. I knew immigrating to a different country would be a good place to eventually deal with a divorce. Oh no, not the 'D' word that no one in the Christian world wants to hear! It is one of the greatest taboos for all ministers and their families. Throughout my young life, the one thing that stayed with me was dad's words, (very strong words that I do not take lightly to this day). 'Do anything in life but do not ever do anything that will tarnish my reputation as a minister.' In my youthful misguided reasoning, I thought I would leave for another country so that I would not hurt my family's ministry and reputation. The damage and hurt I already inflicted on my family would not allow me to go to my parents for help. Keeping in mind the religious, social and educational status of my family, I decided to leave for another country with my then husband. I must admit my youthful pride also got in the way and *['pride' just leads to 'destruction and a haughty spirit led to a huge 'fall'], just as the Bible states in Prov. 16:18.* With much fear, defeat, uncertainty and resolution I systematically planned the divorce, my ultimate failure, away from anyone who knew me or could be in any way impacted by this awful situation.

Underestimating my parents' love and strong sense of parenthood, I thought I could handle things on my own. That too my friends, was another foolish misnomer. It landed me in a long divorce process alone with no support and I had many youthful years stolen from me. It pretty much made a division in my family that was virtually irreparable. The opinion between my parents and siblings regarding this sordid matter differed greatly. Some of them felt and still feel I was unholy and immoral for pursuing the divorce and maybe I am. Many of my siblings love my ex-husband and still maintain friendships with him to this day. The others hurt for me and felt a sense of deep betrayal towards the family and an abuse of trust. Yes, our family has experienced discord and pain because of one misguided teenage decision. We are not immune from family conflicts and hurt. We need to go through these growing pains so that we can be effective ministers to those that are hurting. How can we be empathetic if we have not been in your situation?

One of my sisters reminded me of something that happened just a few years ago. She was going through a life-altering situation and needed my counsel. She reminded me of what I said to her, "There is a reason I went through my life crisis and much pain. It is so that I can help you through your pain". She said this has remained with her because it helped her through the toughest time in her life. I was only effective because I knew what it was like going through a terrible situation. God allowed me to 'stand' through my heartbreak, pain and betrayal; and because I remained standing, I was able to help my younger sister in her time of need.

During my time of divorcement, I experienced self-doubt, a sense of worthlessness and guilt as I faced impending marital failure and the prospect of 'going to hell with a one-way ticket'. My identity and self-worth were intertwined in my role as a wife and caregiver, not my identity in Christ. I thought to myself, that something must have been wrong with me if I could not hold my husband's attention or have a successful marriage. Boy was I messed up. This rejection made me question who I was and whether I had any worth. It made me wonder whether my failure was so horrible that it was okay for someone else, to easily cast me away like a used rag, after years of love and marriage. I could not believe that he did not love me enough to come after me and continue working at the relationship. I questioned my sense of womanhood and sexuality, which are powerful identities that can drown you into a life of despair, if you equate their value to others instead of who you are in Christ. It caused my attitude of mistrusting and disliking people, to deepen within me. These attitudes tightened their grip on my life like evil claws keeping me in the graveyard of a distorted past. It was a self-fulfilling prophecy confirming all the reasons why I should keep people and humanity away from me. This kept an open entrance for the enemy to seed more spirits of hate, lies, unforgiveness and condemnation into my soul. I actually gave evil the 'right' to continue layering themselves into my mind, heart and spirit even though I was going to church. Did you know just as you layer and strengthen truths into your mind and spirit, you could also layer evil lies and condemnation into your soul as well as you spirit? I became everything the apostle Paul warned the Romans not to become. *"For to be carnally minded is death; but to be spiritually minded is life and peace." "But the carnal mind is enmity against God . . ." Ro. 8:6,9" "But ye are not in the flesh but in the Spirit, if so be that the Spirit of God dwell in you. Now if any man have not the Spirit of Christ, he is none of his." Ro. 8: 9.* These lies fueled my already poor outlook on humanity. I have recently discovered that the terms 'guarded' and 'hurt' are just acceptable societal words that allow us to project hatred and bitterness to others. This can eventually lead to a cooling of your relationship with Christ. You may not recognize it now but as you question His love and faithfulness, you begin disconnecting from Him. I allowed my spirit to die *"For if you live after the flesh, ye shall die . . . Ro. 8:13."* He is always with us but it is up to us which spirit we nurture within our hearts and minds. Be aware and diligent to embrace the spirit of love and forgiveness instead of hate and malice; otherwise, you can separate yourself form Jesus when you need Him most in life. The Bible lets us know we cannot serve two masters at the same time. Anyway, my self-doubt threw me into a vicious cycle of guilt and I severed all family ties. I thought I was unworthy and sinful and on and on (kind of like the Prodigal Son). I stopped my childhood routine of praying, reading the Bible and trusting God. When I prayed it was with a bitter and confused spirit but *Christ never left me.* It has taken my entire adulthood and a great pastor for me to realize Jesus never leaves you, no matter how badly you mess up. You do not need to try too hard because 'self' will always lead to failure. God's way is the only way to live and I found that out the hard roundabout way. We cannot live in perfection, as that is God's job. *[Our righteousness is nothing more than a filthy and worthless rag Is. 64:6.]* I was just as much a sinner saved by grace as any other person. Christ is the only perfection. He takes our imperfections and makes something beautiful of our messed up, mixed up lives. That is true Grace and Mercy. God's love for us is pure. We just have to keep walking with COURAGE. As pastor said, [God loves courage. It takes a truly strong person to walk even when people and circumstances beat you down].

One thing led to another and self-debasement, just led me further and further away from the Light, as my soul could not accept the unconditional love my pastor kept preaching about. The ironic thing is, the more I exposed myself to the dark things of this world, God's Light and Truth became clearer and more defined. That is because Light shines brightest in the darkest places and situations. Yes, I explored the things of this world and through exploration found that Jesus is my one true unshakable constant in life. When you have lived all of your life in the fullness of Jesus' Light, world experiences are dark and empty. You know that you are walking in dark places, as God's Love shines brightest in those darkest moments. Loving Light breaks through darkness every time. That is true for the scientific, physical world, the emotional realm and the spiritual dimensions of life. Simply put, light dispels darkness. You truly appreciate God's Light and Love when you have experienced the world's emptiness and soullessness. BINGO! I have just experienced the power of salvation. Despite the families we are born into, we are all sinners and we all need salvation. We must all go through the process of salvation and transformation individually as no one can do this for anyone else. Despite this salvation experience, I still needed to journey through the transforming of my mind and a sanctification process, so that I could release myself from the graveyard of past memories and experiences and move forward to destiny in the freedom of God's love. The pain of the past kept me trapped in captivity, as my mind could not break from the sins of my past, so I could not move forward. I have had to experience Christ's redemption and salvation, just like every born-again Christian out there. That is because we are all born into the sinful nature of Adam, until we experience the rebirth through the final Adam (God's Son, Jesus).

Parents of PKs:

There is no need to bombard young people prematurely with topics of sexuality for which they are not ready. Enjoy your young people, enjoy their youthfulness and zest for all that life offers. Guide within Christian boundaries and allow them to embrace the joys of coming-of-age. Wisdom will keep your children close to you throughout their lives. When alienation affixes itself between parents and their developing children sin can easily distract and lead children to paths of unrighteousness. It is more important to embrace your children to your heart closely and in a haven of safety, rather than pressure them into discussions and issues for which they are not ready to confront. Parents, there is no need to sermonize to your kids. We can easily become immune to your words. Do not forget you have done a good job instilling the Word. Do not underestimate the power of each sermon you preach behind the pulpit. We hear every one of them and we get it, whether we let you know we hear it, or hide that information from you. The sword does cut through the debris of our hearts and it follows us throughout our lifetime. Your words do not leave us but they have life and actually cling to our hearts and minds. Whatever we do, whatever choices we make, those Spirit-filled words cut, pierce and convict us continually. I know from experience that those sermons are life and light in the darkest, and the loneliest of times.

Parents & PKs:

To you parents and kids, I strongly suggest you **talk to each other**! **Listen to each other!** Parents with all due respect, I suggest you talk to your children, not just bark orders as children react in rebellion, when they feel they lose control and you have taken away their right to choose. They become frustrated and they stop listening, tuning you out. This will lead to irreparable damage. Dad was too scared to hear his daughter when I said, "Oh let me go out to the mall or to my friends' house and hang out for a couple of hours and pick me up later". He heard, "I'm coming of age and I want to get away from your control and do irresponsible teenage things". I did not hear dad when he was saying, "I'm sorry honey, I'm scared to let go and turn you over to the world. I don't feel you're prepared for it." Instead I heard, "I am your father and you will do as I say because hanging out with your friends is rebellious and could lead to trouble". He was too scared to hear, "Can I see Gerard at the mall for a couple of hours and maybe catch a bite to eat". He heard, "I want to go out with this boy and have sex with him". I did not hear him say, "I don't know how to slowly let go right now, just be a little more patient with me as I accustom myself with your coming-of-age". I in turn heard, "You will never leave this house with any man or I will break your two legs." Do you see how easily we distorted each other's messages because we listened to each other, with spirits of fear and rebellion? **JUST LISTEN TO EACH OTHER AND REALLY HEAR WHAT THE OTHER IS TRYING TO SAY!** Parents, slowly and graciously, ease your children into independence, knowing that you have equipped your children with tools of the Kingdom. Children it helps if you are patient with mom and dad, as parenting is unique to each child, and misunderstandings will occur. As curiosity drives you, hormones flair up, and you are in the awkward stage of not being a child but not yet an adult, be patient with your parents. You *are* going to grow up and become independent and what seems urgent now, in hindsight, would not be urgent after all. What you think you are missing, in essence is nothing. Taking it slowly may save you from awful life-changing mistakes, like mine.

Marriage for instance, is a precious gift of the union between a husband and a wife. It is like the ultimate union between Christ and His church. When this union is broken and sexual consummation is out of order, a spirit-to-Spirit disconnect occurs. That is because the spirits of both partners become one with Holy Spirit. During a divorcement, I can tell you there is a disconnection from God's Spirit; and that is the loneliest and darkest place for a person. It grieves the heart of God. Here is a little tip, you spend the rest of your life being an adult, but you cannot go back in time to your youth, it is that simple. Maturity has a way of stealing your innocence and it is one of those things in life, you can never get back. You never view the world in childlike wonder ever again. It eventually happens to all of us. No rush kids we all grow up. I experienced one of my sister's heartbreaking coming-of-age and I saw my baby girl grow up, and experience disillusionment, which in turn stole her innocence. I wanted to take away her pain but could not as this was her life decision. This was her journey. She experienced a side of humanity that was dark and cruel. She became an adult at the expense of her innocence. However, she too was able to stand because she had support from God and an empathetic sister.

PKs:

Frankly, guys *'doing it'*, just for exploration is a risky experiment, and there is no emotional gratification. As you listen to sermons on immorality do not let them drive you to *'try it'*. **Think twice and try not to let piety drive you to stupidity**. Personally, I coped with all these conflicts by escapism, music. Find a constructive way to deal with those ranging hormones. I hope you have trustworthy parents who will guide you through these conflicting years. I have heard it said many times by many ministers, that you have a soul tie to any person you have 'slept' with and everyone else who has 'slept' with that person. Those are many souls to have intimate ties with, when you finally find your God-given soul mate. It is a spiritual connection, and a deep dynamic that goes beyond this stratosphere. It is as though you have bonded and become 'one' with another's soul with far reaching, timeless, eternal implications. You really do not want other souls and memories to contaminate a true, pure love that God has for you. Give it time. Let God take care of you. You can enjoy life without sinful acts and rebellious behaviors. I have learned from experience that Jesus is the best gatekeeper of your heart.

Our parents have given us the gift of Jesus and He becomes more precious, as we live each day. There is no need to go the 'Prodigal Son' route, as you will have to go through some type of pigpen experience. By that, I mean one misguided decision could ricochet into a spiritual and emotional downfall, having a domino effect on every aspect of your life. This downward spiral can lead to drug use, alcohol abuse, and promiscuity with devastating results, financial and emotional hardships, loneliness and sinful despair as well as eventual spiritual disconnection from Holy Spirit. Lucky for me I have been able to return to my parents and receive their forgiveness and love, so that I can move forward in Christ without chains of regret to enslave me in past failures, like the Prodigal Son. The following words I wrote in January 1997 can best describe this journey.

> I'm at my first destination
> Just for a while.
> Memories of bygone years
> Flash before my eyes.
> Can't believe the twist and turns
> That have changed my carefree world
> From childhood days on a swing
> To these years of womanhood.

CHS:
I'll look back, just to see from where I've come
And thank the Lord, for all that He has done.
Enjoy the ride, smell a rose along the way
I'll start living the new chapter of my life today.

Found a love from grandfather
For songs and poetry.
Fell in love too early
Left home despite dad's plea.
Several years down the line
Divorced and so confused.
I towed the line paid my dues as
I went back to school

Bridge:
Now I've gotta job, got my education
Found my true love this time.
Turn the page on this old chapter
Write a new one for my life.

Why waste time messing up? We have already been born with a sinful nature, why add greater vastness, between THE MAN and you. Any separation from the awesome connection with Holy Spirit is too great a divide, too high a price to pay when in fact, He completes you. Instead, why not take the intimacy further, higher, closer and stronger, causing explosive increase in the Power of His uncontainable love. Why let the hordes of demons, vomit darkness, depression and despair all over you? (The Vision-The Final Quest and The Call by Rick Joyner). 'Time' is fleeting, speeding by quickly. As my grandmother would say, 'Time is of the essence'. The things you do right now matter greatly in the Kingdom and you are in a literal fight for Life. Preachers' Kids, do not stand for compromise! Be complete in Christ Jesus and do not let the devil steal, kill and rob you of the perfect most empowering relationship with the Creator of the Universe.

CHAPTER SEVEN

FAITH AND PRAYER

I always had a strong sense of faith, reverence and a whole lot of God fear. I prayed every night from my heart (a tradition started by my grandmother). It has been the most precious gift I have ever received in my life. When you cannot even pick up the Bible because you are in a state or guilt and shame you always have, prayer and faith (refer to the story of the Prodigal Son *Lu.15:11:32*).

Here is my real life example. Prayer and faith sustained me even when I was not aware it. Although my prayers were not eloquent or sophisticated, God heard them and never failed to answer me as they reached His heart. As I allowed Him back into my life, he caused practical miracles to occur and turned around my pathetic attempts at independence. Jesus turned me right back around to Him. Jesus preserved my life in the worst of times, when I was alone and desperate. He lighted my way and gave me direction. God reinforced His plan for my life and is strengthening His relationship with me daily. I walked away from Him; meanwhile He was there, waiting for me to return and watching over me with jealous love. He is the prize and the goal and we must keep our eyes on Him. We should focus on our one-on-one relationship with Christ, not people and their behaviors.

My faith now causes me to reach up to Him and pray for an elderly person, knowing He will do a good work. My faith places Him in control and I fill my heart's eyes with the Son. My heart looks into eternity when I set my eyes on Jesus, not congregants, not my parents, not my job, not my husband and not my child. Bottom line whether or not you believe, this relationship is real and it is within you. Face it my friends, this relationship defines other relationships in your life, convicts every word out of your mouth, and makes you conscious of every behavior in this journey. Whether you have experienced a slow insidious developing love or a sudden hot passionate love for Jesus, this relationship is your reference point for all eternity and you know it. It is ever-present and you cannot run from it. There is no other love that is purer, richer or more genuine. Fight it and Holy Spirit will get ahold of your heart whether it happens now or down the line. You cannot run from Him-He blasted the universe into being and He was there with just a Word that had frequency, to cause the beginning of light and life in the universe. So, where were you? He is an infinite God whose creation is finite yet awesome; and He has offered us eternity, to share life forever with Him. Read the book of Job-WOW mind-blowing! God wants to be with us and have relationship so much so, He provided His Son as a connection to Himself, closing the eternal and dimensional divide between Him and ourselves. He wants to spend eternity with us. All we have to do is walk by faith, on the bridge made up of His blood, prayer and His Word. We have God's immediate attention when we start each communication with communion. Let no one take that gift from you and place so much fear in your heart, that you forsake remembering His broken body and His shed blood. Reverence is important but it is our right to partake of communion. It keeps us close to Jesus as we thank Him for saving our sorry states from sin.

Despite the seemingly impossible task, your parents are providing you with the best tool for life. I was a little person trying to find her way in a vast world at a very young age. I had to know who I was at an early age and in whom I believed. I had to be strong and quickly assess the good and bad. Survival taught me how to evaluate whether a person was a 'friend' or 'foe', on a first meeting basis. Today my husband still cannot figure out how it is that my initial assessment of people is so quick and accurate, thanks mom and dad. In retrospect, the journey has not been totally trying and painfully bad. My parents have helped me develop my skill for knowing who are my 'friends' and 'enemies'. Not everyone that says, *[Lord, lord . . . . Matt. 7:21-23].* Just a tip, take it or leave it. This strategy keeps me wise and protected. It is as a 'shield of faith' against the 'wiles of the enemy'.

Preachers' kids are very sensitive to people and the pain they can inflict. We must guard ourselves from falling away in these last days. Today I measure everyone and everything with the Spirit of the Word.

Parents of PKs:

For all you ministers out there keep this in mind, as it will take you a long way. Never expose your family members to the mercy of your parishioners or even other ministers. Be a parent first and take on the role as head of the home, parenting with a firm yet gentle hand. No one should be at liberty to spew out advice at random, prophetic or otherwise to your children. That just confuses them. Do not give strangers parental liberties with you children. Shelter your loved ones and define for your congregation, which of you was *'called'* to service.

Trust in God and in your parenting skills. Trust your children to know true values morals and their heritage in Christ. Having doubts and confusions, questions and curiosities, are the rights of your little ones and your not-so-little ones. They are not always acts of rebellion; it is just the business of living and coming of age. Ask God for wisdom when dealing with your children.

Your only accountability is to bring them up in the fear of the Lord. Remember your children must walk through life, on their own. When it comes down to it, they each have to make their own decisions and they eventually grow up. Trust in your Faith. *"Cast all your care upon Him for He careth for you" 1Pet. 5:7 "Train up your child in the way he should go, And even when he is old he will not depart from it" Prov. 22:6.* Entrust them in God's loving care. I guarantee, no matter where your children go or what they do, they will never depart from **Truth and Wisdom.**

Now that I am all grown up, and have made my share of mistakes, the one thing I have always known, is that God is with me. He chose me in spite of myself and I could go to Him just as I am. God perfects our walk. The walk is not perfect until Jesus transports us to glory. No matter where I have been in life, I have known that my parents were praying me through some touch stuff. I felt it. They did not intrude, although I am sure they would have loved to deliver this 'prodigal daughter.' I did not allow them to rescue me. They watched me (painstakingly I am sure) make my mistakes, stumble through life, work out each crisis, and learn from each of them. As painful as it might have been for them, they stood back as I grew at my pace and in God's time. Have faith parents. Practice what you preach. Live your life with integrity and by the spirit of the Word of God. *Prayer* is the only thing that protects your children as teenagers and adults. Fortunately, my parents learned some of these lessons so that my younger siblings benefited from less harsh taskmasters. Yes, taskmasters are what parents become to their children when pressured by the expectations of others. My parents have surely enjoyed their last two teenagers because they allowed them to be 'girls', 'teenagers' and 'young adults.' Dad became less of a hardliner and more of a parent when dealing with our life situations and so, I too, have been able to call on his fatherly advice but more precious than that, his ministerial advice. My mom's advice has always been practical womanly counsel and in alignment with the Word of God.

Parents, it is more important to have the trust and respect of your children to the point that they **want** to come to you, not only in the capacity of parent, but minister. What an honor to YOUR ministry. It marks a job well done. There is no greater testimonial to your ministry, than when your child seeks your ministerial guidance and counsel. Parents, **unconditional love** even when your heart is breaking, will keep your children close and will bring those children back to you who are lost along the way.

PKs:

'If it ain't broke don't fix it.' If you find fulfillment in your faith in Christ, embrace this wonderful relationship, nurture your ministry and grow in the body of Christ. Why do you feel you have to rebel just because you are bored and have nothing better to do. There is no time to fall by the wayside! The time is at hand and our days are few and numbered. There is no need to take the 'roundabout route' because that is downright foolish! *[. . . Be as a tree planted by the rivers of water that bears fruit in its season . . . Ps. 1:3]*.

If on the other hand you are taking the long way home, do not forget your parents have provided you with skills in faith and prayer, as well as Christian values, lifelines that will take you to a Place of Safety. Remember you can run into The High Tower of Safety and Refuge. God delights in His children and [*He will never leave you nor forsake you. Heb. 13:5]* However, *you* are solely accountable for your actions and you choose your destiny. By default, God is all-knowing and knows your destiny, but life choices are still yours alone to make. Do not think for a second, that careless moments are excusable just because you are children of ministers. Choices are your biggest responsibility, as they have direct and long-lasting outcomes on your lives.

If you are interested in the rest of my journey, I invite you to continue along with me to My Secret Place—*A life Continued.*

CHAPTER EIGHT

MY SECRET PLACE—*A LIFE CONTINUED*
FINDING THE WAY

So, how are things, you ask? What is the latest development? Well, let me see my dad died about four years prior to my starting this writing. My mundane, routine-filled, life (just the way I like it), took a hard but gradual turn towards a different direction. Let me take you back to that last Christmas visit I mentioned earlier in the book. It was the impetus to my transition toward Christ. My dad looked horrible and I knew . . . 'This was it, the last hoorah!' This premonition as it were, only happened one other time and that was, when my grandfather died. I did not want to get all 'spiritual' and 'holy', so I never acknowledged that this was God's Holy Spirit preparing my heart. This 'premonition' (for want of a better word), first occurred when my grandfather's home going was imminent. Again, I was facing the impending death of my dad. Hindsight is 20/20 or so they say. Yes, it was my sweet Father gently dealing with me deep within my heart so that I could bear this heavy, heavy burden in a few short months ahead, in the isolation and privacy of my home. He quickened my spirit just as He did when my grandfather passed. That is the best way I could describe it. Let me explain, the moment I last hugged my grandfather I experienced a deep physical lurch and tightness, in a place between my heart and my stomach, which never left me after that touch. The thought was definitive with no 'ifs', 'ands' or 'buts'. I knew for sure at that moment I would never hold my living grandfather again. The thought was almost audible. I even verbalized it to the person who was standing next to me. I could hear deep within my ear and my spirit, 'This is it you are never going to see him again.' I was experiencing the same spiritual and physical reactions, when I last visited my dad. You see God does not leave us alone. He prepares our hearts. He is our safety net, whether we can admit that or not. He knew I would have to carry this burden a long way and wanted me to 'stand' and not crumble through this journey. When we are still and we take time to listen to the small inner voice, we hear what God is saying to us. When we listen then we can obey and follow His guidance without doubt.

Well, back to the Christmas visit that changed my walk with God. My father was looking like the victim of the grim reaper. He was the personification of death, with weight loss, sunken eyes with underlying dark shadows and frighteningly frail. On Christmas Eve, he made this long but awesome speech about the importance of family, which I referred to in prior chapters. The Holy Spirit (now I can acknowledge this), dealt with my heart so strongly regarding dad's ensuing death that the agony I felt was gut wrenching. During my visit, I calculatedly ensured that I was not physically close to dad or touching him because I would be literally hugging 'death'. This simply was my preparation for what was to come. I was unable to touch and hug my father as I always did. However, when my family said their goodbyes to dad ('papa' to my daughter) on the last day of our visit, I hung back a little. I gave dad the biggest hug I have ever given anyone to date (other than the last time I saw my grandfather). I did not want to let go. I said, "Now dad promise me you'll get yourself to Florida for that angiogram and don't you go dying on me". As the words, 'I promise' came from his lips our eyes locked on each other and we knew this was the last time we would ever hold each other.

Life does not allow us time to breathe or deal with heart wrenching sorrow, grief and loss. Daily routines, schedules, jobs and humanity keep going on without truly stopping and recognizing a person's loss, death and departure from Earth. You cannot believe what my life was like during this time. I had an eighteen-month-old daughter; I was in a graduate program from hell and in the middle of my one of my internships. God was preparing my system for the shock and the comfort I would so desperately need. Time was getting closer. Three months later, I got a call from my sister who was crying and explaining that dad insisted on getting on the plane even though she begged him to get to the hospital at home. He was supposed to have gotten medical attention in Florida. I think he did not want to die at home. I got in touch with my sister Danielle in another state and told her to get on a plane and immediately meet dad and mom in Florida, as I was in the middle of my useless internship. Unbelievably, Danielle and I made this plan prior to dad even beginning this trip. We discussed the possibility of an emergency occurring and a possible game plan should that occur; as we would be the geographically closest children to mom and dad. She instantly flew off to Florida and within twenty-four hours, I got the 6:00 a.m. call. 'Dad's gone he just died'. Oh no, I was not even there! My poor sister totally traumatized by the hospital experience and my poor devastated, lost mom, I thought! The logistics were poor as I was unable to get to my mom and sister. I did not let her repeat the phrase because I knew he died when that phone rang. I calmed her down, provided as much direction on the phone to help her deal with this crisis. We formulated the best game plan to deal with mom. Mom a strong warrior in the Lord also has human frailties and weaknesses. She became the woman that lost her soul mate. She needed comfort and guidance. She needed love and patience as she experienced the pangs of being a widow. She too had to find her way. She needed healing and ministry to her body, as she too became very ill after her loss. I needed to be a minister to my mom. Even though we knew where dad was, the loss was still great and mom felt the loss of dad deeply. Like all families, we too needed a time to mourn and a time to grieve.

Well after the initial call, I orchestrated at long distance, how the family members were to get each other to the family house to break the news. All the while, I was numb. After the drama of dealing with my hysterical family, I went home for the burial with my system in shock but resilient. To this date there is still unsettled business affairs, the horrible split of my family (oh yes even pastors' families have issues of greed, jealousy, misplaced anger and resentment). We are still working through this death with lots of scars, hurts and pain. The shock of this loss was so deep, sudden and unexpected for the family and someone needed to take control. When I got home, the nightmare was in front of me. There were tons of visitors paying their respects and not quietly. There were services outside of the house with a loud microphone and blaring speakers. There were people, many, many people. To this day, I do not know who organized that situation but it was unbearably crowded and noisy. I could not hear myself think. To be quite honest it was a horrendous fiasco.

Somehow, my siblings even the ones who are ministers, were scattered and did not know how to deal with the grief. God set my heart in order for this short time. On the day of the viewing of dad's body, the family came over to the family house, but could not organize themselves. This upset my mom and she started to cry. All of a sudden, I heard myself tell the family to gather around in a circle. I called them to attention and prayer. Could you believe it, God used me, the lost sheep of this tribe. You see no matter how far you think you are from God, or how far you think you have run away, He is still with you and unshaken by your silly pride. The family's nervous energy became still just as Jesus said, '*... Peace be still...*' *Mk. 4:39*. As I provided counsel and direction regarding the mourning process, there was silence, peace and reverence. Holy Spirit moved in and allowed the family to grieve in order. After I prayed with the family, my sister in law came up to me and said she could not believe I could pray like that. She said I should be in ministry. I told her 'I am' because God chose me before I was born. What made her think I was not in ministry? Could it be because I was one of the kids not standing behind the pulpit preaching or involved in the church organization? Kids, never forget from where you come and who you are in Christ Jesus. In whatever role or job you find yourself, you are always a minister first to others because He has chosen you!

At the death of my dad, I became as a lost little girl. I did not know where to go or how to find my way. All of a sudden, I underwent an uncontrollable inward panic attack, 'I did not know what to do with my life.' Well that is what it felt like when dad died and I am sticking to it-no philosophizing no spiritualizing. I could not concentrate, I could not think and I could not perform any of my life's roles. I did not know why I was on the earth, 'was it to live and die and be judged by this Perfect judge that will cast me into Hell because I was just 'being'. I became so busy with the business of living, meeting the bills, taking care of the family and becoming a professional I lost my purpose and destiny. I thought, 'was I made to live and then just die, is that it?' 'No it can't be', I kept thinking to myself over and over again. I knew the answer in my head but I needed to reconcile it in my spirit. Meanwhile to my husband, I appeared hard and cold, distant and in control and we stayed away from references of daddy in daily conversations. He was so good just letting me 'be' and only acknowledging comments regarding dad if I initiated them. We went on living but I was barely surviving and unknown to anyone around me I was sinking deeper and deeper into depression, panic and chaos with no organization or focus. All of a sudden, I found myself going through the motions with my husband and child, with a numbness that I cannot fully explain. I completely fell apart all by myself without anyone knowing. Once again, I shut out the world and dealt with life alone.

To be quite honest my reason for living was now dead. I was only attending college because dad told me to do so and emphasized that all children, especially girls, should have a solid education and income. All of a sudden I was without my soul mate, my confidant, my rescuer, my stable rock, the one man on earth to whom I could bare my soul and not be judged, the one I could trust, the only one who could make me laugh until I was senseless. He was a gentle friend. Yeah you are right, I was not aware of it until it hit me like a ton of bricks. I was very dependent on my dad and trusting him instead of God. Actually, he was god in my life. Upon his death, I learned some difficult and unexpected life lessons so here they are listed below.

Just a little tip to pastors out there:

Attention ministers organize your affairs! Business is business. Your family will need money, a home, a trust and a Will so that they do not have to deal with discord amidst the grief. Make sure your congregational business, finance and leadership, are outlined in a Will; or the congregation will become as lost sheep looking for leadership wherever they can get it. Leaders instantly become greedy and feel a sense of entitlement. Trust me . . . the stories I can tell will leave you startled down to the core. Do not mix or confuse the parish house with your home affairs. Have a home for your family outside of anything related to the business of the church. Be a good steward of your family and congregations. I thought a little pinch of truth would increase your awareness and sensitivity. Do not be gullible into thinking people will be kind toward your family after you have passed. People are cruel with private agendas. Worse of all they try to achieve these hidden agendas when under the guise of being supportive to the family during transition; 'wolves in sheep's clothing', to coin a Biblical phrase. Moreover, do not think family members would be kind to one another. Family members become greedy and feel entitled to something, anything whether there is an estate to inherit of not. Fierce fights within the family circle become the order of the day and you see behaviors of malice and greed that are unexpected from those closest to you. Have business affairs in place.

PK's

God is a jealous God. I am not saying God took dad away but look at the idol I made of dad in place of my sweet Heavenly Father. How could I do this to Jesus? I was not even aware that dad was my idol! Meanwhile Jesus got his face crushed beyond recognition, spewed blood from every inch of his body, nailed to a cross, had a crown of thorns smashed into his head and lost His Father's love. He went through all of that pain and loss, just so that He could reconnect with me and gain my love and attention. He put Himself through agony, so that I would not have to go through any priest or intercessor. He gave me total access to The Father, The Source of all Life. How did I return His love for me, I put all my trust in a man-wow! At the time, I could not deal with this whole aspect of spirituality. Remember, I have started this account with hindsight, so I can acknowledge this now. Wow, I do sound preachy like a preacher man's daughter huh! Watch out I'm comin at ya guns blazin.

CHAPTER NINE

A ROUNDABOUT SEARCH

I found myself embarking on a quiet and private journey to find my dad. I was brought up in church so could you believe this, I wanted to desperately find dad, me a Christian believer, was I nuts!

Oh but I had to find him at all cost, even knowing there is a separation between the physical, earthly body and ethereal spirit. I have always known there is great divide between the two different dimensions. It is amazing the extremes to which sadness will take someone who cannot let go of grief. It started with an obsessive curiosity of wanting to know, where in the stratosphere dad was and what was he experiencing. Off I went full steam ahead, delving into books and documentation on life after death and near death experiences. God allowed me to move in this direction until I found Him and trust me; He made sure this dunderhead was going to run into Him and crash into His loving arms.

While reading, researching, exposing myself to new age concepts, time travel, out-of-body accounts and meditation type books I ended up safely in the arms of Jesus-smile. Thank God, He protected my mind and spirit from the occult, which tantalizes and seduces. God protected my mind and my pathetic, searching, yearning heart. What I have discovered along the way is that, I had been yearning and searching for God all this time. I was longing for a completeness, which I could not fulfill unless I took time to develop a spirit-to-Spirit relationship with Jesus. I have discovered that it is ultimately about each of us entering into a true intimacy and love relationship with Jesus. In order to help others discover who Jesus is, one first has to discover Him for oneself. Books have a great way of pulling you into a quiet world of discovery, knowledge and imagination. There are all sorts of books out there dealing with topics ranging from mindless romance to the different disciplines of science. There are 'how to' books and books on religion, spiritualism and the occult. My grandmother always said, 'words have life' and good or bad words have a life all their own. They can sway you, seduce you, correct you, enlighten your path, educate you and even confuse you. Whatever they bring to your mind, remember words are alive. The access to any subject is vast in a world of advancing technology so remember God's Word is Truth. Not all knowledge is Truth. God is Truth He is the Word and he lived among us. Be careful where you search for Truth. He is the only way to Truth.

While searching for your answers guard your minds and find Truth in the Word of God. *"You will find me when you seek me, if you look for me in earnest. Yes, says the Lord, I will be found by you . . ." Jer. 29:13 &14.*

PK's:

We all take different paths during this journey and oftentimes get lost along the way. Just remember *[He will keep that which has been committed unto Him against that Day. II Tim. 1:12].* God has to keep His Word to your parents to keep you *'against the Day'* and at all cost. He is unchanging and so are His fundamental words of Truth. When you *choose* to find Him, He will gently guide you through the maze, so He can be most relevant to your heart's longing.

My searching, readings and delving led me to a place of discomfort as I realized that all that I have been searching for was with me all the time. Let me explain, during this literary journey, I discovered that we start with Jesus in Heaven and He wants us right back where we started before birth; that is, with Him and in Him. After countless hours of reading I realized, all experiences by those who crossed over to the other side and returned, reported meeting the Creator who is Light and Love, even if they were on their way to Hades. They all reported Love, transcending all things, people, places and time. It was in the Word all the time, why did I choose to miss it! The Bible describes Him as waiting for us with open arms. All He has ever wanted is our love and adoration, so that He can love us back. Even when we do not even think about Him, Jesus is holding us and loving us with His loving kindness and tender mercies. The simplest illustration is this, when my daughter is not thinking of me or even mad at me, I keep on loving her. Whether she is on a play date, sleepover, at school or her many activities she is constantly on mind and I am thinking about her lovingly. I cannot wait for her to come home so I can hug her and hear her tell me she loves me and missed being away from me. Meanwhile she is too busy growing and exploring to think of me. Nevertheless, she is always on my mind and in my heart. Like my daughter, we too are just too busy with our lives. We are 'busy about nothing' (another Maism), to notice that Jesus is quietly waiting for our embrace and declaration of love. After all, it gives Him pleasure to pleasure us, His ultimate creation. Imagine this, before the creation of anything he made provision for us to come back to him freely, straight into His presence with no interferences, no obstacles and no intermediaries. There is no fear as Jesus became our perfect redeemer and has covered us with His protective blood.

It is simple kids, God made us in His likeness and image to worship Him and have sweet communion. He wants relationship with us. He made a fail-safe way for us to have an awesome, radical, boundless, supernatural, mind-blowing, limitless multidimensional relationship. In rediscovering that dad is in the Throne Room with all the wonders of Heaven and its glory, I experienced increasing restlessness, emptiness, and identity crisis deep within. I was excruciatingly aware of my spiritual numbness. I just could not accept that, 'this life is it' and I am just going to live out my days and then die and go to hell, for being in a state of 'nothingness'. The Bible tells us that God would prefer if we were *'hot' or 'cold' than 'lukewarm'.* Let us check out ***Rev. 3:15, 16 "I know thy works, that thou are neither cold nor hot: I would thou wert cold or hot. So because thou art lukewarm, and neither hot nor cold, I will spew thee out of my mouth."*** That is a big loser reason for God to say, ***"... depart from me ..." Matt. 25:41*** folks, isn't it.

Here is my thought on the matter and my interpretation or misinterpretation as it were. He might perceive the state of being 'lukewarm', the most arrogant of behaviors. Let us stop and think about it for a minute. If you are *'hot'* for Jesus, He can take that drive, intimacy, enthusiasm and heated relationship and continue perfecting the interpersonal relationship to unbelievable dimensions. Using your intimacy with the Creator can expand His Kingdom and grab lost spirits from the one that steals and destroys. On the other hand, if you are *'cold',* it is your choice. He will try His uttermost to ensure you have all opportunity to experience His love. He will pursue you with the passion of a lover as well as the love of an unrelenting father. Then you can actively determine whether you choose to reject Him, and never behold his Face and His oneness, for all eternity. If you recall, the worst part of Jesus' cross experience, was the moment the Father turned His face away from Him and rejected him. If you are a parent, then you know God's sacrifice and Jesus' ultimate sacrifice, to restore direct and limitless communion with us. Think about it, can you do this to your child for the love of another? To turn away from the child you love the most to save another who does not even love you, or choose not to acknowledge your existence, that is great love.

Lastly, we have '*lukewarm*', middle of the road people. You feel arrogantly competent to take control of your own life and steer it according to what you think the course of your life should be. You do not go out of your way to hurt others, you mind your own business, you feel okay about yourself, you think you are a good person and if anyone is offended by you or your lifestyle, you don't really care. You can even justify indulging in sin as long as it does not hurt anyone. You think you are okay in your skin and other people should not be watching your life, your family, your money or your business decisions. You think you are self-accomplished and you do not need the Almighty dictating anything to you. You think you do not need direction, or purpose from God because you are doing it by yourself and doing a pretty darn good job of it. Can you see why He would think this state is the worse state in which one can be? You feel your sins and little indiscretions are not affecting others as long as your life remains private and quiet. In fact, you feel you are your own god. This is the most arrogant of all the sins because you feel you are bigger than God Himself. You do not need Him for anything. You have ascended. Whom does that sound like, not just a little like Lucifer? This is just a reality check. I know I have you pegged as this fully describes you.

Many preachers' kids get into this lukewarm zone and think they are okay, just by association to their parents and their parents' ministry. Well think again. You do not get a free pass to eternity because of parental association. You are responsible for your careless behaviors, preacher's kid or not. This describes my experience and probably yours as a preacher man's kid. I hope this raw expose makes you seriously think. Anyway, this started gnawing at me. I thought, I can no longer go on feeling numb and without purpose, nor can I continue with an incomplete and empty spirit. For the first time, I took a close look at myself through the mirror of eternity. I found myself in the awful state of being '*lukewarm*' and an entirely offensive spirit to my Redeemer. It is from this point I threw myself into my spiritual awakening from wasted years of slumber.

CHAPTER TEN

I WANT WHAT DADDY HAS OR DO I?

In an incidental way, we have gained access and insight to the 'death experience' and we have caught glimpses as to what happens on the other side. This has been largely an unknown until people started having near death experiences and returning to the land of the living, due to advancing technology. I have read that, upon time of death people immediately float or rise out of their bodies and into eternity, so death as we know it is not death but as I like to refer to the experience, **life transitioned**. From all the reading I did, it seems as though the spirit transitions into a dimension of ever after, eternity so to speak. It seems that at the last brainwave and heartbeat, the spirit is alive and hovering, seeing everything. Realizing that the spirit is free, it needs to do something about that. You see, none of these research books and biographical stories were far fetched to me, as science has a nasty way of reviving the dead, when these persons should be on their way to infinity, to The One Who Was and Is and Is To Come. People have described time of death as a transition, a float, a walk, or propulsion to the Light from the confines and limitations of the body, and into a continuum of eternity, with absolutely no boundaries of time. I know this sounds a little science fiction but just think about it and keep reading. So the spirit becomes free to surpass speed and time and be present, appear, materialize, at the precise moment of conscious thought. There are no time restrictions, no dimensional confinements and no need for gravity. Best of all the spirit is in that place of continual worship, glory, perfection and Love. Oh, I thought to myself, that is what it means '. . . *to be absent from the body is to be present with the Lord . . .* 'Cor. 5:8, radical! Wow! Just writing about this blows me away. It makes me wonder why I did not become a physicist or scientist-you see kids there is a lot about God that is awesome and waiting for you to explore! We need great Christian minds in science and education; so go for it and become a great mind and person in the Kingdom, I challenge you!

Why is it, at age forty-seven Biblical passages are clicking in my soul, I do not know. Suffice it to say, it is just my time. Maybe the men that I loved, who made me feel safe, and secure had to leave this world so a void could be created, then once created I would seek the Almighty. I do not presume to know. Gradually it seemed, yet all of a sudden, I found myself wanting Jesus to fill me up full force and full glory. I never felt such a spiritual void before. I began yearning for the One that could complete me in Spirit and with Truth. I wanted a refuge for my tired soul and weary broken spirit. So I kept thinking, 'how can I reach you Lord, really touch you without having to die'. It seemed that all the people who encountered God in an awesome way had to die. I have since learned that the soul-man has to die daily. Well this yearning came from some deep part of me and I became very aware of my spirit's hunger as I began searching in my own way. I wanted God to be my reality and not some doctrinal statement and dead faith with religious nonsense. Turns out, I have come to realize along the way, that dad is in Heaven and is being intimate with God from his level of relationship with the Almighty.

It turns out dad's God or perception of God as was his level of relationship, would not be mine. It is not that God is not the same righteous first person of the Godhead; it is just that He is dynamic and relevant to each of us, as He needs to be. By that, I mean our experience with God is multifaceted. We perceive Him as though looking through a diamond cut mirror. Dad would have met Jesus in Heaven from his level of relationship and perception he experienced Him on earth. For example, if dad passed away knowing God as a Savior to all Mankind, he entered Heaven at that level of intimacy and understanding. From there he would keep on experiencing, learning, evolving and perceiving Him with greater dimension, clarity and perception throughout the eternal realm (read Anna Rountree's Heaven Awaits the Bride). It is cool, to know that you can know even greater secrets and keep growing in intimacy with The Eternal One!

PK's:

By the way, did you know God is also known as the Ancient of Days-wow are you blown away yet? He is so awesome! Do you realize if we had all eternity with the Ancient of Days, we still would not be able to fully know all there is to know about the Creator! We will always be increasing in intimacy and knowledge of who He is and our perceptions will continue to increase and change in depth, in length and in width. It turns out my daddy's God is great but He is presenting Himself in a different, dynamic way to me. Guess what, my dad's God is not my God. By that, I mean that the fundamentals remain the same but I am experiencing him with a different perception, intimacy, anointing, knowledge level and mantle. He is a warring God, a returning Captain, my last day Champion and my eternal King! He is an intimate lover unlocking end time keys of the kingdom and downloading revelation to activate his Kingdom on the earth.

Our God is relevant to our 'now'. The music, the instruments, the worship, the medium of the message, the message itself is new wine and we are new skin. We are presenting the same fundamental gospel, with relevance for this end-time season. We are facing different social and spiritual issues with greater magnitudes never seen before. Christians are experiencing transportations from place to place, visitations from earth to Heaven, and shifts in spiritual atmospheres. We are a different generation experiencing God in a different way but He never changes. He is just working faster with a greater momentum, 'the latter rain outpouring.' I am sure my daughter will experience God in a different generational relevance than I experience Him today. My daddy's God is not my God yet *[He is the same yesterday today and forever Heb: 13:8.]*

CHAPTER ELEVEN

UNLIKELY PLACES

I spent many hours reading and discovering that dad was experiencing awesome continual spiritual wholeness, and everlasting peace. I thought to myself, 'books you have not failed me yet so I will just keep on moving forward in my search to find the 'missing'. After all, I found out where dad was and got a glimpse of what he was experiencing and instead of thinking of him as dead I began celebrating his life up there, the fact that he has won the prize and he is now witnessing everything from the perspective of eternity. I began celebrating his beginning, the first day of the rest of his life. This searching led to a place that is unconventional yet not so surprising, in an era of advanced technology.

So unbelievably, I went on the Internet to find God, I know it sounds flaky and crazy. I have some Bibles at home but I did not go there for some reason. I started searching for God, who He is, how could I get to Him, how can I hear from Him, and how could I feel and touch Him. Oh yes the preacher's daughter went searching for God, unbelievable I know, controversial and weird but I did it. I came up with some bizarre sites but the Lord teaches if we *[persistently look for Him we will find Him. Jer. 29:13]*. For me the journey still continues and is an ongoing dynamic relationship. I found Him on the Internet, online documents, e-books, websites and precious Christian books. Who says He is not out there. If you look hard enough, you will find Him. If you have an earnest yearning and deep desire to find Him, He will lead you to the places you need to look. He will guide you to Himself. He used the Internet in a logical inspiring way to help me find Him. He respected my space and my need for privacy through this part of my journey. To be honest it was shameful and embarrassing trying to find Jesus after all my years of religious indoctrination. I wondered what people would think if they knew. Boy would they laugh at me. This was a time to hide and search without distractions and interferences. You see, knowing about Jesus and having an intimate relationship with Jesus are two different things. Jesus guided me, (and still is), to those things that were comprehensive, things that needed clarification. His Spirit has been inspiring my heart, increasing my knowledge and motivation.

Let us go back a bit. While searching, things got crazy at work and I became run down and weak. One day I was just standing on my husband's boat and bam, my ankles went out on me, I fell down dead weight and broke both my feet, talk about a freak accident! I was out of commission for three months. I was thrilled actually as there were many transitions taking place at work and I needed time to pursue God and now I had it. I spent hours on the internet searching for Jesus, listening to sound bytes and video clips, reading documents and listening to interviews of supernatural encounters. I sifted the [chaff from the wheat]. I eventually found this one book with big bold letters FACE TO FACE WITH GOD by Bill Johnson. 'Ah ha' just what I needed to know, a how-to book on how to find God and make the connection I longed for. Amazon books did not fail me. Now I will find the One that I have watched everyone else find but I could not, for some reason. The author of the book is a preacher's kid too with a huge ministry in California. What a coincidence! All of a sudden, I was out of work for three months, physical therapy and daily challenges. Guess what, it was the best thing that happened to me as I was reaching a turning point in my search. I had TIME, yes time to focus on this very important connection that would grab my spirit from an eternal death. Not only did I read this man's book and listened to him on internet video clips, I took a plane towards the end of my recovery and told my husband and daughter I'm going to California to the twenty-four hour Prayer House. It was good, refreshing to be there for three days but I think I should have stayed in the Prayer House longer and fasted more. As good as the visit was I still missed the mark. Actually, I was just a little discouraged after taking this trip of faith. I did not come back empowered and on fire and performing miracles. However, I was unaware that God started a good work within me and set His seal deep within me, giving me an insatiable hunger for His love and relationship.

PKs:

These days I often wonder why *our population* (preachers' kids), give up our gifts, heritage and souls to the devil's control so easily. We simply hand over our control and our soul-man to him without a second thought. We just allow him to destroy our eternity and our relationship with Christ. We literally *choose* to give up our relationship with the Almighty because of emotional pain, disappointment and rejection. Why is it okay for us to allow complete darkness to violate and overshadow our lives and our love for Jesus? What is the physical, carnal payoff? The way I see it, it is as though a King has given us all the riches and power and we turn them away and say 'no' I'd rather be powerless and poor. I accept the ugly costume jewelry instead of the beautiful diamonds. Do you know that you find the most beautiful diamonds under great depths of the earth? These gems form under great pressure. That is what you become when you 'stand', after the battle and the fire of words, condemnation, finger pointing, gossip, malicious intent and betrayal by others. There is absolutely nothing in this world: material possession, temporary fleshly cravings, power, or riches that appeal so strongly to my carnal or spirit man, that I would willingly trade for eternal torment. There is no pay-off so tantalizing, that I would trade the sweet communion with the Father for shallow, counterfeit experiences. Is the pay-off worth it for you?

Let me share this, in case you did not know, **you are the ones the enemy wants the most.** The chosen, the pure in spirit upon dedication, the high priests of the Almighty, the ones empowered to go out and share redemption with the world. You are God's delight separated apart from this world. I know some of you are exhausted trying to find Him amidst the religious system. Is it so hard, tiresome and discouraging that you cannot go the extra mile, to receive the ultimate Love that the Father so willingly gave to you? Let me put it to you this way. Ask any treasure seeker, what is the best part of getting any treasure? He or she will tell you that it is the experience, the joy, the struggles, the journey and the unexpected adventure of finding the treasure. Well that is what it is like for me at this moment and in this season.

Anything worth having is worth finding. Just think about it guys, do an inventory of your life. I am sure that every earthly thing you have, has been worth the hard work and the sacrifices because of the fulfillment and happiness your possessions bring you. Now think of this on a forever scale. Can you wrap yourselves around the magnitude of this matter? I have found that this journey of finding Jesus becomes transforming. His Spirit is so all consuming He cannot be contained. He is the biggest high you will ever experience, He transcends any trip you can ever experience and He takes you to supernatural journeys your mind cannot conceive. He can transport you to realms of glory that are unimaginable than any drug-induced fantasy. More importantly, there are no hurting aftereffects of coming down from your trip or experience with the Creator. He completes you when you fully commit to Him. All you need is to remain vested in worship and keep your mind and spirit attuned to His frequency. That is because it is all spirit-to-Spirit connection. You are connecting to the Spirit of the unlimited, all-powerful one true living God, the Almighty. Right now, all I can tell you is that He is true to His Word. God says to us, *[You will call on me and pray unto me and I will hearken unto you. And you will seek me and find me, when you search for me, with all your heart] Jer. 29: 12, 13.* Heaven has provided us with the pattern for intimacy and connection. Just throw down your crowns, your sense of self, your accolades, your trophies, your flesh, your pride, your opinions, and your body like the elders around the throne. When you do bow get low even lie prostrate. Then, like the angels that surround the throne just love on Him. If you do not have words, try [holy, holy, holy, to the One Who was and Is and Is To Come . . . . Holy, Holy, Holy]. Shut out the world see Him high and lifted up, then let Him consume every inch of you in all His beauty. Soon your spirit becomes one with His, Heaven invades earth and earth intertwines with Heaven. After this intermingling, He reveals your destiny and purpose. It is that simple yet complex in meaning and dimension. Let me share more meditation songs I wrote during these worship sessions. They are simple, precious heartfelt words to Jesus.

> I wait for You, with patience and in prayer
> Lover of my soul, harken and come near.
> Let me see your face, feel you warm embrace
> Let me know your voice, Lord, so that I'll obey.
>
> Another goes like this:
> I bring glory, honor
> I bring glory and honor and Pow'r.
> I bring glory, honor
> I bring glory and honor and Pow'r.
>
> To the Father and the Son and the Spirit
> I bring glory and honor and Pow'r.
> To the Father and the Son and the Spirit
> I bring glory and honor and Pow'r.

Nothing fancy just words of love and worship to the Lover of my Soul, the Creator of all and the Father who is always with me.

CHAPTER TWELVE

MY DISCOVERY OF JESUS

My ongoing walk in Faith has taken me over the course of forty-eight years and counting. God has been many things to me. His personality and qualities have changed as my perception of Him has shifted throughout the years. From childhood to present, I have gone from learning that God was Love, a Good Shepherd performing great miracles while on earth, to a terrifying God who would send me to Hell if I stepped out of line. Yet again, He has transformed Himself to Lover of my Soul. Conversion so to speak, if you like to think of it as that, seems to have been an ongoing process from childhood to adulthood. I remember how He tugged at my heart at a tender age preparing me for His Love and intimacy. My siblings and I would 'play' church. My brother could preach just like Evangelist Billy Graham, we could sing like the great gospel singers, and we could be the most spirit-filled enthusiastic charismatic congregation you could ever witness. We could even speak in tongues, like 'the crying-laughing lady' in the church my dad used to pastor. Somewhere within those pretend services and alter calls Jesus was revealing Himself to us. He would visit us and we would feel Him in our hearts. His Spirit would yield our hearts to Him and we knew we were His, play or no play. The effect of conversion has recently taken hold of me in a gentle and gradual way after many years of rebellion and restlessness. I wanted to explore Jesus on my terms in my own way and on my time schedule, too young to realize a person does not always have that luxury in life. He has been patient with me. I wanted him after I experienced college independence 'Room 222 style' and single female, apartment living 'I'm gonna make it after all' Mary Tyler Moore style. During this time, I was unaware of the loving salvation process. During a lifetime of running, I did not realize that I was actually searching for Jesus. I have not had an explosive moment of salvation, a miraculous healing from some incurable disease, there have been no visions or sounds from Heaven but just a gentle steer in the right direction. It has been a lifetime search for The One who has always been with me all the time. It reminds me of the lyrics of the chorus of a song by Gary Paxton "He Was There All The Time" It goes like this.

He was there all the time
He was there all the time
Waiting patiently in line
He was there all the time.

In my search for Jesus, I have been experiencing greater clarity, intimacy, and completeness, as I find little nuggets of who He is, along the way. Those little nuggets change my dynamic with Him, increasing intimacy during worship. I can tell you for a fact that getting there is half the fun. With each new special revelation, I soar upward to another realm of intimacy with the Lover of my Soul. Salvation has not been this big huge bang for me but this patient, slow insidious father-child relationship and lucky for me Christ has allowed me time to grow and discover who He is. Somehow He has tolerated my rebelliousness, my tantrums, my questions, my bad behaviors, my doubts, my fears, my hopes, my dreams and my roundabout search for Him. It has been a gradual and abiding relationship and He has been the one constant. I am glad he has kept me on an elastic string and kept pulling and tugging at my mind, heart and body, keeping me safe and protected. He was watching over me all the time, even when I did not want his attention. Salvation has been a gentle and eventual override so to speak. Here is the best way I can describe it. Holding on to words of life and eventually accepting salvation, is beautiful. I wrote a song called 'Gradually'. It was how I eventually experienced salvation so I will share the words with you.

"You came into my life one ordinary day.
Didn't know the exact time or place.
At the start just a form, not to stay
'Till your love in a gradual way,
Caught upon the strings of my heart"

Your love leapt out at me from your Word
As I read with congregation that verse
For God so loved this old sinful world
That He gave His One begotten Son for us.
To die on that rugged tree from sin.
A King-how could I repay Him?

CHS:
Now I've a song to sing and a life to live
'Cause I've found in you my Lord
A release for my longing soul
And a lifelong peace from this old sinful world.

PK's:

This is the best way I can explain it. I am giving up control of my mind to Jesus. I constantly have to submit to the mindset of being totally open, fully yielded and completely abandoned to the control of the Holy Spirit and the love for humanity. My spirit and my soul become completely satisfied each time I steal away with Him. After acquiring another insight from reading the Bible or other religious texts, I then notice that my understanding deepens as I speak to Him using that additional truth. In other words, I get into my hideaway prayer chamber for an intimate encounter with my Lord. This handmaiden bows before her Lord and unbridled praise and worship begin. Every new truth is added and layered onto my worship repertoire and enriches my communication with my Lord. I speak more sweetly to Him; and my soul becomes increasingly aligned with my spirit, in recognizing the unfathomable majesty of God. This then results in stronger and more effective prayer, intercession, faith and worship. My head stops getting in the way, so to speak and my spirit takes over my mindset. It is in this way breakthrough to open heaven is happening for me, and the meaning of that distant scripture that says *[. . . The effectual, fervent prayer of a righteous man avails much] James 5:16* now makes sense. Now as new truths layer my knowledge, *[I can pray and sing with the spirit and with understanding, deepening my communication with God. 1 Cor. 14:15].*

I trust that you can see how this is coming together for me! It is happening slowly and insidiously, creeping up ever so unexpectedly, like a gradual wave about to crest. I simply use increased knowledge and understanding from the Word, to expand my worship and intimacy with Christ. The new truths I learn from God's Word changes my perception of Jesus and increases my knowledge of who He is. Therefore, I speak to Him with greater insight. Like any relationship, the more alone time you spend with your loved one, leads to awesome passion between each other, and closer intimacy. The consummation of the human mind and spirit to Holy Spirit is realm blasting, as He reveals powerful secrets through the spirit of His Word. Like any consummation, there is a slow joining, an all-consuming bonding and a love explosion. To have this with the Creator of the Universe is wild! This time is precious and should be guarded and consistent, for it is in this place the Creator reveals His deep secrets, His awesome love and hidden truths. We my friends are *joint heirs* with Christ we are not 'autonomous' as one kid stated on a television show. The Godhead of the Universe has joined us to Himself so that we serve and govern with Him as joint heirs and in sonship. It is in that knowledge we are independent of earthly limitations and boundaries. It is only then you can walk in the supernatural Love and power of the Supreme, causing eternity to accelerate its miracles into our Now, and our Time, explained by Renny McLean. God has designed you by His will to worship, so that you can be as kings and priests unto Christ. To be autonomous is to be satanically influenced young people, as that is how Lucifer fell. This attitude makes you god-like and self-sufficient. You belong to Jesus, His rule, His power and most importantly, His awesome Love.

CHAPTER THIRTEEN

THE JEALOUS CALL

I think this is the generation experiencing Jesus with greater outpouring, stronger manifestation, and liberating revelation from His Holy Spirit. Jesus is more dynamic in daily lifestyle at work, at home, at school and in our spiritual walk. One evangelist put it perfectly, [this IS the last season and we have to keep ourselves from falling away and reach the prize because there are no more chances]. Grace and great grace is for the taking now. Renny McLean on his CD Awareness of Now, lets us knows that time is ending. He gives us wonderful insight as he states, 'Time is Eternity's child.' When it was put that way, things got a whole lot clearer for me. He explained that [time is coming to its end and 'eternity' is overtaking 'time' therefore when we speak in faith, our supernatural miracles and events, are manifesting on the earth in an accelerated manner.] This is the last hour you are living in kids. The devil knows it, so he has sent out hordes of demons just to reckon with you. He must steal you from God's army now. He has to ensure that he keeps you down because you are 'chosen', you are strong in battle strategies and warfare but some of you are too rebellious or too young and immature to know it. The devil has to be sure you remain broken in these times or you will literally take souls away from him and from eternal death without fear, in the name of the Lord. The sad thing is, these demons do not even have to wage full war on your lives, they just have to employ shoddy strategies and take cheap shots to keep you down. Look around and see how many of our brothers and sisters are lost and dying along the way. This is your wake-up call. Maybe you think you are autonomous but that is a cheap lie of the devil and a way to keep your soul trapped in eternal death. My friends Eternity and life in eternity is catching up with you. Just in case no one ever dared tell you, autonomy is arrogance, which will lead you into direct defiance with The Living God. That my friends, is a place no one should be. I strongly suggest, *'The fear of the Lord is the beginning of wisdom . . . Ps 111:10.'*

PK'S:

We are the generation at war and we are His end-of-days warriors. It matters where we take Him! Take him daily to the people you are exposed to, with strategy and wisdom. He is leading us into battle, to grab souls from the devourer. We are a mighty army to go into battle, with Christ the Captain leading us there. We have a great foundation of truth, knowledge and preparedness. You my friends are more prepared than you think. I am coming out of the place you are in right now. There is no more time to let people, things, emotions or situations, keep you from entering the Kingdom or define your eternity. Do not give them the power to steal an awesome intimate relationship with limitless riches and heavenly boundaries. You are the chosen ones kids! I will tell you how I know.

Go back to your growth and development class. Do you remember seeing film and hearing a narrator say, only one sperm will be the strongest and fertilize the egg? Before that point in time, He knew it was you, only you. He was there all the time just watching over your creation. The strongest out of millions became the one unique creation, you. All bets were on you before conception. He knew your name and the person you were to become. God knew who you were going to be, before you were born. The Almighty God chose you-what an honor *[For many are called but few are chosen for His pleasure Matt. 22:14].* From inception, you have been strong, so rise up, Oh ye children of the Highest, Melchizedek Priesthood—CHARGE! Attack lives that are drowning, dying and being destroyed because we are too busy deliberately getting lost along the way. Shake off the slumber and the slothfulness and rise to the ultimate call of a battle ALREADY WON. You are in an army you are not independent, nor self-directed. Let Jesus take you to a relevant place so that He can become your God, your lover, your friend, your Light, and Life. Have a love fest that is mind-blowing and revolutionary. Let your dynamic love relationship be relevant to YOU and your ministry. Make no mistake kids you do have a ministry! He wants you and you know it.

The Secret Place is your alone time with the Father, the love of your life. Worship as the angels in Heaven and bow down low. Submit to His perfect Love. He will complete you. Take the time to get quiet before Christ and create time in your daily routine to love on Him. You are all He wants and He will love you right back. He made us to love Him. The infinite Creator who is beyond time, the all-consuming Light (God) will consume your being and make you one with Him. Imagine being within God's uncontainable, untamable greatness, purity and Light-phew! How restful is that! What an adventure with the Great I

AM! All that I can tell you is that I have a deep sweet clarity of God's love that I cannot let go, I am not letting go. Jesus talks to me in my heart, I feel His awesome presence as I kneel, His Spirit intertwines with mine and then He leads me to His living dynamic Word. Here is my experience when I bow.

> I come before You, with uplifted hands
> On bended knees I bow.
> I lay prostrate, before the great I AM
> Lord you're the object of my love.

> *CHS:*
> My breath of life you are my joy
> The longing of my heart's desire
> Entwine Yourself in me, oh Lord
> Love of my soul, take pleasure in me.

> *Bridge:*
> I run into my secret hiding place, with You the Most High
> Sweet communion while wrapped in your embrace
> Sharing in You Glory, face to face.

He is the everlasting I AM. Jesus has made himself tangible and real to me, in a deep spirit-to-Spirit bond that no one can ever question. He judges in mercy, love and with much grace, so that we are perfect in Him. Like the song says, "He gave His life what more can He give . . .". What else can He do to show you how much He loves you? He is **Absolute,** he is your friend and alone time with Him will cause you to say *[who can separate me from the love of Christ Rom. 8:35.]* When you have experienced the amazing love of Jesus, nothing can keep you from daily intimacy with Him. It reminds me of the scripture that says, *[not tribulation, distress, famine, nakedness, peril, no sword no principalities, nor powers, no height, no depth, life nor death can separate us from the love of Christ. Rom. 8:35-39].* Whether you accept Him for who He says He is, whether you believe in His Word, whether you choose to pursue this supernatural relationship, or whether you rationalize Him, He remains **Absolute.** God is in love with you and all of humanity. He always sees you through the blood of His Son Jesus and you are in perfect sonship with Him. You do not have to do anything to make yourself worthy because you cannot. He has done it all for you, just approach Him within the covering of Jesus' blood. Nothing you do buys His redemption it is what He has done for you. You are worthy to approach the Creator through His Son, Jesus.

CHAPTER FOURTEEN

THE UPDATE

Could you believe it is September2011? Here I am still editing and working on this small piece of work. I started this in September of 2008. It has taken me all this time to write a few pages not enough pages to call this writing a 'book', as my husband recently and jokingly pointed out. It seems to be more of a tiny little booklet with a lifetime of condensed experiences, intense actions and reactions and developing spiritual awareness. After three years of writing about these accounts, I hope this will be cohesive, productive and dynamic to you the reader. Well it is not about quantity but quality. I feel as though this might be the time to release these thoughts as I have changed and grown for the better since the first chapter. You have probably detected changes in attitude, and purpose as the book has progressed and transformation has evolved and overtaken my life.

I am sure the raw honesty, anger and hopefulness will grab my PK friends who are in depths of despair or confusion. I trust Holy Spirit will somehow use these unsophisticated words to grab at your hearts. This is the time! The Kingdom will soon be with us in its eternal fullness and 'Time' will cease to be. You have been in my heart and prayers for many years as you have suffered violence. You are the frontline victims and warriors. I know you may have deep hurts from people who are supposed to be spiritual family. I know coming-of-age and all its conflicting feelings cause stress, strain and pain. I know manmade, religious dictates can oppress you, causing you to lose your childhood innocence. I know societal and peer pressures can close in on you. I know this may be a time for you to make many decisions while you are plagued with feelings of uncertainty.

PK's:

Run into your hideaway closet your Secret Place and breathe, breathe in the pure air of Heaven. As the war rages with greater intensity, the enemy wants you and I cannot just sit back and let him have you. A watchman should never sleeps. There is continual and ongoing war for your souls and your eternity. You are **WANTED** and the enemy never stops plotting your eternal torment. There is a continual fight for your eternal disconnect from the life-giving Light. It comes subtly and in the form that is most hurtful and closest to you.

Many of you PK's deal with abuses of all kinds. Some of you deal with abusive parents who are to supposedly God-fearing but you cannot tell anyone. Many of you are confused as your parents deal with marital abuse, conflicts, indiscretions and divorces. Some of you may be seeing your parents engage in corrupt behaviors yet continue to stand behind the pulpit preaching the Word. PK's out there you may have parents that preach holiness and your parents may subscribe to pornography and other unscrupulous acts. You are dealing with identity crises, sexual confusion and addictions of all kinds. You are silent and hurting because the enemy knows how to shut you up and break you. It is okay to get help, reach out to the Savior and all the wonderful Christian resources now available to you. Be brave my friends God wants you to be encouraged. ***Deu. 31:6 says, [be strong and of good courage, don't be afraid of them, the Lord thy God will go with you and not forsake you].*** He will, ***[lead you in paths of righteousness for His namesake] Ps. 23:3.*** Just trust the Lord, and do not let anyone turn you away from Jesus. He is more precious than gold. Take a good look in the mirror. It is just a mere reflection of your outward appearance. Jesus sees you He truly sees you, the real you, your soul and your spirit. Your black lipstick your spiked multicolored hair, your leather jackets, your chained clothing, your tattooed skin and your multiple piercings, do not shock Him. He loves **YOU**! You cannot hide behind a painted façade because He has already bought you with His blood. Your behaviors do not intimidate Him because He is God. He created you and saw you eons ago. Your rebellious behaviors are no smoke screen as He knows your heart, He knows your soul, He knows you, the real you. He hears your heart's cry. He sees and knows all things. ***'For the eyes of the Lord run to and fro throughout the whole earth, to shew himself strong in the behalf of them whose heart is perfect toward him . . .' 2Chron 16:9.*** No matter where you are or where you think you might be going, He has you in His arms. His love has you fixed in His heart, my friend. Your journey is destined to wind up at the starting point of Love. The mirror image you think you are projecting does not mean a thing to Jesus. He loves you, piercings, tattoos, promiscuity and all.

This would be worth writing, if it takes just one of you, out of the enemy's dark worldly influences and lies that undermine this most important relationship. Do not sit on the fence of indecision, right is right and wrong is wrong. Do not compromise God's love and truth.

Do not let church politics and evil lies steal your eternity and doom you into a life of eternal separation from your Creator who loves you. You can never be of this world because your destiny is not here but in the eternal love of Christ. That is why you are restless and you feel you do not belong, because you do not belong to this world. The world is temporal and passing away quickly. Your upward journey toward the Groom should leave a permanent trail of God's Love that lost souls can follow.

Meanwhile I challenge you my friends, to break through to open heaven and experience the treasures laid up for you. Praise and worship are the keys to unlocking Heaven's doors. You are the **doors** through which the Lord will enter into your life on earth and you can experience Heaven on Earth. You may be wondering what I mean. *Well Ps. 24:7-10 tells us, [Lift up your head o ye gates; and be lifted up you everlasting doors and the King of glory shall come in. Who is this King of glory? He is mighty, strong in battle and the Lord of hosts.]* You are the medium through which Holy Spirit binds you to the heart of the Jesus and moves through this world, for Kingdom change. Your Secret Hiding Place is where you will find your fulfillment and empowerment to journey without distraction. Your Bridegroom wants you to focus on Him and only Him. If you focus on Jesus, you will not lose your direction nor become blindsided by people and the crushing cares of this world. In fact, you will become a world changer as lives change when you share the love of Jesus. Jesus always prepares your heart for the journey, within the Secret Hiding Place, a place just for you and He alone.

Remember The Secret Hiding Place is a place of peace and serenity, a place of praise and worship and a place of Holy supernatural war. In this place, you cannot be proud and arrogant before the Mighty One of Israel. How can you, when you bow and lift you face and hands before the Messiah? When you bow, you humble yourself under the mighty hand of God. You immediately have the attention of the Father, as it is a position of humility and acknowledgment of His infinity. You are immediately giving respect and letting Christ know that you see Him as all knowing, all-powerful and ever-present. Have you ever tried having a one-to-one conversation with someone more powerful than you are? Have you ever been the one sitting and the other person was the one standing? It can be humbling if you needed to be assertive.

You would have to take a more offensive posture to assert yourself in the conversation. Well unlike the world's model, your most effective posture is to bow, as it will gain the attention of God, immediately. It makes you present yourself and your requests from a position of reverence, instead of arrogance and self. It is one of the secrets of your Secret Hiding Place.

It is good to honor Jesus by remembering His sacrifice and Love for you. Any lover likes acknowledgement. Once in a humble posture, woo His Spirit closer by eating of the bread and drinking the wine both representative of His sacrificial love for us on earth, His death and resurrection. When you approach God with honor and reverence, you gain His immediate attention. Honoring the other person in a relationship binds you to that person. This is communion. Communion starts your conversation with Christ on the right foot, so to speak. He really likes the posture of a humble and thankful heart. I find that this act further seals the unity between Jesus and me. It purifies and sanctifies you before the Almighty. Communion protects your prayer time with Christ so that the enemy cannot distort communication with the Father. His blood seals the interchange from Earth to Heaven and back to Earth.

It is more effective when you fall on your face. By that I mean lying prostrate before the Throne. When you prostrate you *[present your bodies a living sacrifice unto God, which is holy and acceptable unto God]. Ro. 12:1.* This posture lets Christ know that you are surrendering fully to Him and the communication and intimacy grows. You may be thinking, why this posture? You are allowing Him to delight in you and have His way in you, without reservation and pretense. You do not hold anything back from God when you are lying flat on your face with arms outstretched. In that way, Holy Spirit can unite your spirit to His Spirit. In this posture, you allow Him to relate with you openly and honestly, without limitations and hang-ups. This shows Him that you are not trying to cover up anything in your life. It lets Him know that you are openly and honestly approaching Him. The first thing Adam and Eve did, was hide. You cannot hide from the Lord. He sees all of you but He needs you to acknowledge this truth. This means (like any relationship), you *trust* Him with your heart and your life. You trust Him not to hurt you, you trust Him to protect you, you trust Him to *lead* so that you can follow, you trust Him to hear you and you trust Him to take care of every aspect of your life. This becomes revelation. These are the mysteries and the wonders in The Secret Hiding Place. This leads to a most offensive attack against the enemy. *A posture of humility leads to intimacy with God, which is an offensive position in the spirit world.* Let me share what happens to my praise and worship, when I posture myself on my knees, or lay before the Lord.

> I bow before you, O Lamb of God
> In your Presence, I humbly bow
> With thankful heart, I bring my praise
> For Your redemption, for the life You gave
> I bow before You, Ancient of Days.

> Holy, holy is the Lamb
> Worthy to the Great I Am
> You alone deserve all praise
> You alone are King of kings.

> *Bridge:*
> I sing Holy, Holy
> You are Lord God Almighty
> Forever Holy, Strong and Mighty
> Holy, Holy is my God.

Lastly, I have found that when you transition from praising Him to worshiping who He is before the Throne, revelation and truth begin to envelop your spirit. He is so phenomenal, fast, and huge. Depending on the intensity of your worship, you may receive many truths and revelation, and you can miss some of them. It helps that during this precious prayer time, you have a notebook and an e-book or hard print of the Bible. When revelation manifests you can only accept it and not always fully process its message or content entirely. Writing down these truths, allow you to go to the Word and find confirmation, and expanded knowledge. The Bible begins to speak to your heart and mind. The message becomes dynamic and alive as you explore God's Word. The message from the Word comes to life in your heart, through Holy Spirit. He uses His Word to clarify the nugget of truth you have received during your alone time with God. The Bible expands the message from Heaven. The Bible is the only way to understand the depth of the revelation, because God's Spirit has inspired each word. Only His Spirit brings life to the Word. It also allows a person to determine whether the revelation is truth or error. *[. . . And it is the Spirit that beareth witness, because the Spirit is truth." There are three that bear record in Heaven and witness on earth for the Father, the Word and the Holy Ghost are one]. 1 Jo. 5: 6, 7.]* Simply stated the Word validates your revelation during prayer time. That is because Jesus is the Word, the living dynamic Word of Truth that sustains you and me.

Your relationship with Christ is not rocket science people. The above has somehow turned into my quick 'how to' to get to the Savior. I hope this helps you in some way. I also trust that these thoughts keep you from traveling on some of the roads I have traveled. Until now, there has not been a practical guide to reaching my Creator. I have discovered it is simply about investing in a relationship. Like any relationship, set aside time for your beloved, honor Him and worship Him until your sprits unite. As this unification happens, explosion occurs. After this, the supernatural encounters and communication take place. As you meditate on the revelation He gives, you will be surprised how God will use you to be relevant to someone in need. The far-reaching effects will be mind-blowing.

Congregants, Preachers & PK's:

I hope my experiences and this simple guide to exploring your relationship with Christ will encourage you to approach the King, your friend. I trust my experiences will cause you to stay on the path that is narrow and focused on Christ. It is my heart's desire that if a brother sees another falling by the wayside he will go to the fallen one, pick him up, bind his wounds and minister to him in love. I trust that this will cause each of us to guard our hearts and our tongues and none of us will be quick to judge the other. Let us not forget the Good Samaritan, *Luke 10:27-37.* Did you know Jesus commissioned us to do the same? How about it folks could you imagine how much greater our outreach could be if we would just minister to each other in love, bind up the wounds of those that are hurting and provide the message of healing and redemption at each person's point of need! We would spend less time in counseling sessions and more time in praise and worship as the [greatest of God's gifts is Love] 1Cor 13:13. Just see Jesus in others then love can flow from Him through you to them. During today's meditation, these simple words were sent to me from the Creator.

> I see Jesus, pure and Holy
> Full of beauty, so divine
> Lord you're radiant, in thy Glory
> There is warmth, in Your Light.

I hope that at the risk of opening up my imperfect life to you, with all its failures, mistakes and redemption, you will see a little clearer as you journey towards Christ. I trust with all of my heart, that you will avoid costly spiritual pitfalls along the way. During this journey, I discovered at great personal cost, we do not have to sit in the seat of the scornful, dance with the ungodly, become drunk in places of darkness, indulge in reprobate thinking or defile our bodies out of frustration, confusion anger or self-pity. I have written this at a great personal cost to my family and me. I trust however, it will bring much healing to you my brothers and sisters in the Lord. It is my prayer that these simple words unite the Bride of Christ, and His Holy Spirit will complete the good work He has begun within you. Be courageous and step upward, as Jesus lights the way for all Preachers' Kids who journey on *A Road Less Traveled.*

BIBLIOGRAPY

1. America Standard Version. *Kindle Bible—The Holy Bible,* formatted for the Amazon Kindle, (Jan. 4, 2010, pub.)

2. Tyndale House Publishers, Inc. and Youth for Christ/USA, *Life Application Bible The Living Bible* (Wheaton, Illinois), 1988.

3. *Thompson, Frank Charles, D. D., PH.D., comp & ed., The Thompson Chain-Referenced Bible. Fourth Edition King James. Version.* Owen, Frederick G., D. D., Ed.D., arch. B. B. Kirkbride Bible Co., Inc. Indianapolis, Indiana U.S. A., 1982.

4. Joyner, Rick, *The Vision The Final Quest and The Call* (Morning Star Publications, North Carolina, US, pub. 2000). Previously published Joyner, Rick *The Final Quest,* 1996, 1997. Joyner, Rick *The Call,* 1999.

NOTES

Referenced Books

5. Johnson, Bill, *Face to Face with God. Charisma House, August 2007*

6. Rountree, Anna, *A Breathtaking Glimpse of Eternity-Heaven Awaits the Bride. Charisma House A Strang Company. 2007 (Christ Jesus Triumphant, Inc., U.S.A.)*
   Previously published as The Heavens Opened 1999; The Priestly Bride 2001.

7. Costello, Robert B., D, editor in chief. *Random House Webster's College Dictionary.* (Random House New York, 1991).

Referenced Book Titles

8. Hardy, Thomas, *Far From the Maddening Crowd 1874.*

9. Forster, E. M., *Where Angels Fear To Tread.* 1905

Lyrics Quoted

10. Kaiser, Kurt *1975 copyright. Oh How He Loves You And Me*

11. Author, Lord You Never Turn Your Back On Me, I'll Look Back, *Gradually, I See Jesus, I Bow Before You Oh Lamb Of God, My Breath Of Life. I Bring Glory and Honor and Power. Unpublished*

12. Paxton, Gary *1975 copyrighted. He Was There All The Time.*

CD References

13. Renny McLean, Dr. "Awareness Of Now" Global Glory copyright, 2010.